Digital
Legacy Plan

Digital Legacy Plan

A Guide to the Personal and Practical Elements of Your Digital Life before You Die

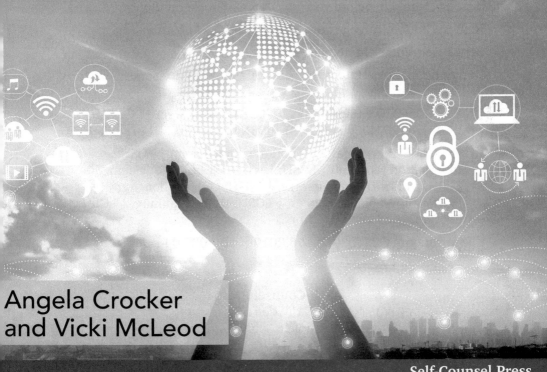

Angela Crocker
and Vicki McLeod

Self-Counsel Press
(a division of)
International Self-Counsel Press Ltd.
Canada   USA

Self-Counsel Press acknowledges the financial support of the Government of Canada for our publishing activities. Canadä

Printed in Canada.

First edition: 2019

Library and Archives Canada Cataloguing in Publication

Title: Digital legacy plan : a guide to the personal and practical elements of your digital life before you die / Angela Crocker and Vicki McLeod.

Names: Crocker, Angela, author. | McLeod, Vicki, author.

Series: Self-Counsel reference series.

Description: Series statement: Self-Counsel reference series

Identifiers: Canadiana (print) 20189066822 | Canadiana (ebook) 20189066830 | ISBN 9781770403109 (softcover) | ISBN 9781770405004 (EPUB) | ISBN 9781770405011 (Kindle)

Subjects: LCSH: Personal information management. | LCSH: Information retrieval. | LCSH: Legacies. | LCSH: Social media. | LCSH: Online social networks. | LCSH: Online etiquette. | LCSH: Biographical sources. | LCSH: Estate planning. | LCSH: Executors and administrators.

Classification: LCC HD30.2 .C76 2019 | DDC 025.04—dc23

Self-Counsel Press
(a division of)
International Self-Counsel Press Ltd.

| Bellingham, WA | North Vancouver, BC |
| USA | Canada |

Contents

Notice to Readers

Laws are constantly changing. Every effort is made to keep this publication as current as possible. However, the authors, the publisher, and the vendor of this book make no representations or warranties regarding the outcome or the use to which the information in this book is put and are not assuming any liability for any claims, losses, or damages arising out of the use of this book. The reader should not rely on the authors or the publisher of this book for any professional advice. Please be sure that you have the most recent edition.

Dedication

Written in loving memory of our angels:
Alex, Beryl, Marie, Stan, and Yvonne.

Acknowledgments

Our writing partnership would not have been possible without Rebecca Coleman to introduce us. We feel fortunate to have Rebecca's wisdom, support, and donuts in our lives. We thank her, and chef and author Nathan Hyam and the wonder of online connection for bringing us together.

In turn, writing would be impossible without the loving attention of our husbands, Paul and Ian, and Angela's son, Sean. They feed us, nurture us, and love us every single day. No matter how many words we write. Angela's father, Brian, is her biggest fan, online and off. We thank him for his endless enthusiasm. Vicki is grateful for the ongoing love and support from her mother, Beda Martin, and her siblings Etanda Morelli and Peter Laurie. Every day we get to share the planet is a blessing and a joy.

Thanks also to our amazing editor, Eileen Velthuis. Her enthusiasm and encouragement make writing a delight and her guiding hand can be seen in every page of this book.

We'd also like to acknowledge the generous support from our classmates at Simon Fraser University. While writing this book,

Vicki completed The Writers Studio program with a focus on narrative nonfiction. A special thank you to her mentor, author JJ Lee. Meanwhile, Angela completed her Master of Education degree with her education technology and learning design (ETLD) cohort.

As women who live our lives both online and offline, we are delighted to have a diverse and supportive digital family, especially our friends and colleagues at Social Media Camp in Victoria, BC, Canada, who champion our work year after year.

Thank you to our peers in the digital space, many of whom generously shared their wisdom and opinions on digital legacy planning: Bosco Anthony, Ms. Candy Blog, Fred Armstrong, Danielle Christopher, Steve Dotto, Megan Fox, Tara Hunt, Nicole Johnson, Cynthia Lockrey, George Plumley, Sylvia Taylor, Shirley Weir, and others who prefer to remain anonymous. A special personal thank you from Vicki to Ann Wilson and Joseph Onodi, for cheerleading and text messaging her across the finish line. We both thank Faye Luxemburg-Hyam for her unflagging support and endless wisdom.

We would also like to acknowledge that we work on the unceded territories of the Coast Salish peoples; particularly the Kwikwetlem, Kwantlen, and Katzie First Nations. We thank them for the honor of writing from this beautiful land.

Introduction

One hundred years from now, there will be 1 billion dead people on Facebook. That's a sobering thought for each of us as we consider our own mortality. While it can be uncomfortable to talk about death, it's important to prepare the personal and practical elements of your digital life before death. In this guide, co-authors Angela Crocker and Vicki McLeod offer solutions for the practical, social, emotional, and technical aspects of your digital legacy. They include best practices for online memorials, social media and mourning, and digital etiquette in death. Tools and resources are included throughout the book to help your digital estate planning and empower your estate's executor.

From online banking to decades' worth of digital family photos, copious creative or intellectual property, or personal history documented on social media, everyone has a widespread digital footprint that tells the story of our lives. How much of that story remains online after we're gone? Who has access to banking, passwords, and important digital records? What about painful or deeply personal elements of your personal or professional legacy? In life, you have the opportunity to make choices about your digital legacy. If you don't, you risk your legacy being misinterpreted, lost, or simply becoming digital litter. It's time for a digital legacy plan.

Together, we're here to guide you as you explore your digital legacy plan. Every plan is unique yet there are common themes and elements that are universal.

Vicki provides a perspective based on many years as a certified personal and business coach and as a leader in the human potential movement. Having worked intimately with hundreds of people, Vicki understands that human beings have a handful of core desires — to have a sense of belonging, to feel creatively fulfilled, and to feel that their lives have mattered. The search for meaning is a deeply personal one. As we age, or start to consider the end of our lives, the subject of legacy becomes more important. Vicki is also an advocate for expressing authenticity in all that we do — online and off — and has been a leading voice in the world of ethical social media and digital marketing for using the internet mindfully, and finding a positive human balance between our digital and analog lives. In her book *#Untrending, A Field Guide to Social Media That Matters: How to post, tweet & like your way to a more meaningful life* (First Choice Books, 2016) she asked us to consider the legacy inherent in our social media posting habits and online behavior. She urged us to take a long view of our online engagements and how they impact the lives of those around us.

Complementing Vicki's wisdom, Angela's professional work centers on communication, community, and education. With more than 25 years on the internet, she has lived through many shifts in our digital lives; from fax to email, from newsgroups to social media, from dial-up to Wi-Fi. Her work is grounded in academic studies in mass communication, print and online publishing, education technology, and more. Drawing on that knowledge, she teaches digital life skills to help individuals and businesses navigate the online world. Ever curious, Angela is a chronic researcher seeking to experience and understand how humans communicate and connect, how communities are built and maintained, and how technology plays a role in it all. At one time, she had more than 450 unique social media accounts open, mostly for research purposes! She's especially interested in the affordances of technology that improve our lives while also advocating our right to decline technology and stick with analog solutions. Like Vicki, she is a pioneer of ethical social media. Angela first wrote about digital legacy planning briefly in her book, *Declutter Your Data: Take Charge of Your Data and Organize Your Digital Life* (Self-Counsel Press, 2018), a topic that resonated with readers and required further resources. In collaboration with Vicki, this book fills that need.

Philosophically, we are aligned in our steadfast belief that everyone needs a digital legacy plan. Let us be your guides as you explore new, and potentially tender, territory.

Throughout the book, you will find a variety of resources and worksheets to help you. Blank copies are available in the download kit included with the purchase of this book. We recommend you print and date this material as you work with it. Additional resources are also available, particularly the "Death in the Digital Age" group on Facebook, a community facilitated by Angela and Vicki where you are invited to share your process, ask questions, and hear what others are doing.

1. What Is Digital Legacy?

A legacy is anything — material, emotional, or digital — that leaves a lasting effect after we die. Many think of this in terms of the material goods typically described in a last will and testament such as your house, your car, your jewelry. It's also familiar to think about the emotional legacy we leave in the people who survive us — children, friends, colleagues — who remember us with love or respect or anger. Your legacy is also reflected in your body of work, or the impact you have had on the world around you. What will you be remembered for? Digital legacy is a modern extension of what we leave behind when we die.

At first glance, digital legacy might be mistaken for the technology that houses our information. Computers, mobile phones, cloud storage, and more store gigabytes or even terabytes of data in a compact package. But the real digital legacy is in the data files themselves. Some files are practical things such as financial records, land title documents, car ownership papers, custody agreements, medical details, and life insurance. Others are professional documents such as contracts, reports, databases, and client records. Additional files may be creative endeavors. Poetry, music, drawings, photography, or the novel you never finished writing could all be part of your legacy. Personal writing, too, can be left behind whether that's a diary, gratitude journal, correspondence, or vision board. Your digital legacy goes beyond the files in your technology — think of your social media accounts, playlists, viewing history, podcast subscriptions, and more. Collectively, all this information and more is your digital legacy. What does your data say to the future?

2. Who Needs a Digital Legacy Plan?

This guide is for anyone using the internet to transact business, manage accounts, connect with loved ones, or engage in social media. Unless you are a celebrity, large brand, institution, or corporation that already has strategies in place to deal with legacy planning in all its forms, including digital, this guide will be a valuable resource.

Perhaps you are a solopreneur or an entrepreneur with a small business. You will find this guide a helpful companion, used in conjunction with strategic business planning. It is important to safeguard your online assets, both financial and intellectual. You will want to have a plan in place for transition or succession, should something happen to you or a business partner.

If you are a rising online brand or influencer, you will want to consider the transfer of digital resources, social proof or trust, and credibility and reputation in the event of your demise. Your digital assets, whether creative, or as part of marketing and sales funnels, have value. Hopefully, the fans and followers you have amassed are a vibrant community of ambassadors for the brand(s) you represent. They offer leverage and power in the marketplace. What have you done to protect ongoing revenue from online products or services?

Our friend and colleague, Steve Dotto of Dottotech.com, is a well-known media personality. A few years ago he decided to move his brand from traditional television and radio mediums to the internet. He has rapidly become internationally recognized in digital circles as a YouTube and technology expert. Steve has a vast collection of excellent videos and online courses, as well as a significant community of patrons on Patreon who contribute monthly to support his content creation. He has developed successful online marketing and sales funnels and generates significant revenue resulting from the trust he has built with his online community. What happens to these assets once Steve is gone?

There is much to consider for those of us doing business in the digital environment. If you are a writer, visual artist, filmmaker or videographer, blogger, musician, or other creative artist, you may have finished or unfinished creative work-in-progress stored online. You will want to carefully consider what happens to your original work once it is in the hands of your estate. What about royalties from existing or posthumous works?

For example, *Digital Legacy Plan* is Angela's fifth book. Her work will no doubt stand the test of time and will continue to be published. She is also a prolific digital content creator. As mentioned, in the course of her research, Angela has opened more than 450 social media accounts for research purposes. While she's made significant efforts to declutter her data, she'll likely have research-in-progress that will need to be managed by her digital steward after death (in this book we use digital steward to indicate the person who will oversee your digital legacy). She will need to consider the fate of future royalties as well as what her estate should do with her unfinished or unpublished creative work.

Working professionals are likely to have transition plans in place if they work for others, but it is important to think about digital assets you may keep on home computers, in your personal phone, or in filing systems outside of the corporate purview. What happens to them should something happen to you?

Our friend, Fred Armstrong, works at a senior level in local government. If he needs to do work from home, he can use a work laptop, or access his desktop remotely, and work in the city's ecosystem. If something happens to him, the IT department can access his files through their shared document management system. If your workplace or organization doesn't have this kind of system in place, what happens to your remotely generated work-related data?

If you are a professional with your own practice, for example, a medical, financial, or legal practitioner, you must think about transition plans. This applies not only to the running of your practice and the role of staff, but also to the management of client files and important records. While Vicki and her husband were preparing an early iteration of their personal wills, the notary they had hired died. The McLeods were unable to access the records or copies of their draft documents. Ironically, the notary did not have a plan in place and left a mess behind. The McLeods were forced to start from scratch.

In the process of researching this book, we conducted a survey of our peers working in the digital space. From content creators to technical experts to digital strategists, this group lives and works online with great skill and solid know-how. When we asked if they had digital legacy plans for their data, 50 percent reported that they had digital legacy plans in place while the rest did not.

We also asked the same group if they want to live on digitally after death. Fifty percent indicated that they want to live on digitally while the rest of the group added questions or caveats to their potential digital future. One wanted their professional legacy preserved while another sought to secure intellectual property. Others wanted the majority of their digital assets deleted and some haven't given the issue any thought yet.

While this data is drawn from a convenience sample, we believe it is a strong indicator of the shifting considerations for us all as we live increasingly digital lives.

Consultants and other contractors need to think about client files and ongoing project work. Who on the team has access to the important information and can pick up the ball, or pass it along should you no longer be at the helm? Is any of that information proprietary or privacy sensitive? If so, it will need special attention.

Vicki and her husband Ian are partners in business and in life. They have a limited company and hold share certificates. They work closely with clients at the senior levels of organizations and much of their work is of a sensitive and strategic nature. In addition to the legal considerations of succession for their corporation, they need to consider safeguarding sensitive client information and have transition plans in place for important projects. As well, in her work as a personal coach, Vicki needs to have a plan for private client records and communications.

Professional considerations aside, nearly everyone who has a computer or mobile phone has amassed a substantial collection of personal (possibly private) data. From family photographs to personal records, after your death family members will need to decide what to keep and what to delete. Direction from you, while you are still living, will be invaluable to them. If you are married, your spouse will seek and be grateful for anything that soothes his or her grief. If you are a single parent, your child or children may need to make these choices on their own. If you are childless, your estate executor or other next-of-kin will be called on to deal with these decisions.

Are you in the business of death? We are thinking here about funeral directors, insurance brokers, notaries, estate planners, and others who may work with the dying, the bereaved, or those who are planning their estates. We hope you will keep a copy of this book handy as a reference. Better yet, buy copies to offer to your clients as a resource. We say this only slightly tongue-in-cheek. The information you will find here will be invaluable to your clients.

You may be someone who doesn't see what all the fuss is about. After all, you'll be dead, so what difference does it make? You are right, it may not make a difference to you, but it will make a difference to those who come after you. Even simply conveying the attitude "I don't care what happens to my digital legacy after I die" will be helpful to your loved ones.

Of course, given the subject of this book we urge you to be more thoughtful and pragmatic in your approach. What we hope is that you will consider your own specific circumstances and give serious thought and planning time to what will become of your digital presence in the same way you plan for the more tangible aspects of your estate. Take the tools and tips we offer and apply them to your unique situation. Your digital legacy plan can take any form that works for you and your digital assets. This might be a simple letter stored with your will. Or maybe it's an extensive document that you email to your executor and/or digital steward. The worksheets you'll complete as part of the exercises described throughout this book can also be bundled to create your digital legacy plan. You can save hard copies, scan them into a PDF, or both. You know best what your needs are, and who is most likely to have to take care of executing your wishes. Plan with them in mind.

If you are the executor of an estate, or you are simply a friend or family member who has been left with the task of sorting through a lifetime of accrued digital "stuff," this book will better equip you for a difficult task. We'll provide you with concrete steps you can take to sort through what is important and why, and also respect the emotional process and toll this kind of administration can take.

3. Why Digital Legacy Planning Is Important

Digital legacy planning is important for many of the reasons listed above. For entrepreneurs, artists, and other professionals it offers the following:

- Ease of business transition and succession.

- Continuity of important or confidential client or corporate work.

- Transfer of hard earned social proof and follower trust.

- Preservation of personal or professional reputation.

- Protection of intellectual and creative property.

- Strategy for online revenues or valued marketing and sales systems.

On the personal side, digital legacy planning empowers you to determine for yourself what your personal legacy will be, at least online. It encourages you to start now with the thoughtful consideration of what you choose to post about yourself, your family, or your business, understanding that these posts could well outlast you. Hopefully, digital legacy planning will inspire you to think about how you choose to engage online, with social media, in comment threads, or as a content contributor. This kind of planning puts you in the driver's seat in terms of designing your online legacy. Making these choices now means your loved ones won't have to do so later.

Failure to plan may mean that others may be left with a mess to clean up. Assuming that those dealing with your estate will be grieving, adding the additional burden of sifting through years, possibly decades, of accumulated data simply isn't fair. Adding to that, your loved ones will need access to important data you have stored in order to fulfill your wishes. Making it easily accessible to them is an act of love, one you can perform now, while you are living so that it will be easier for them once you are dead.

To help you create your digital legacy plan, we've designed a series of worksheets that correspond to the various topics throughout this book. You'll find completed samples to illustrate how to use each worksheet in the relevant chapter. From naming your digital steward to passing on your passwords, the worksheets will prompt you to provide the necessary information. Blank copies are available in the digital download kit included with your purchase of this book. See the end of the book for instructions on how to access the download kit. If you complete some or all of the worksheets, your digital steward will be better informed about your digital footprint, your digital wishes after death, and your digital legacy.

1
Overcoming the Taboo of Death

Digital legacy planning means we must consider for ourselves, or for those we love, the reality of mortality. In order to deal with the practical and personal elements of digital life before death, we must overcome our discomfort with talking about death and dying itself. Particularly in western cultures, this discussion is largely taboo.

As we enter these discussions, it is important to seek and find comfort, and to understand the resources, online and offline, that are available to help with the conversation. This book is one such resource. There are others, and as our global digital footprints grow, people the world over are considering the implications of, and potential for, dealing with death in the digital age.

1. Accepting Our Mortality

Approaching the topic of digital legacy planning is made more challenging by the very human tendency to avoid thinking about, or discussing, death itself. Part of the challenge is simply a kind of denial. The younger you are, the more challenging this will be, and interestingly, the younger you are (that is, born after 1985, the dawn of the internet) the more likely you are to be working, playing, and creating in the digital space. There is a certain irony here.

At the same time, if you have picked up or downloaded this book, you are aware of your own mortality, or dealing with that of a loved one. If you are past middle-age, in the second half of life, perhaps you are just taking a peek at your own mortality, seeing the glimmer of your own finish on the horizon. It is possible as well that you are simply a very practical and pragmatic soul and you realize that death is in fact inevitable, and as with coordinating a vacation or buying a house, planning pays off.

No matter your age or personality, most of us share a certain discomfort with the topic of dying. We consider it morbid. Talking about death and dying with our friends or loved ones invites a certain kind of energy into the conversation. It is the energy carried by grief, laced with an anxious sense of foreboding. Talking about death can be scary.

The conversation around death is also an intimate one. It requires us to sit face-to-face, looking into the eyes of our beloveds, acknowledging the very temporal nature of our life here on earth, and theirs.

In her moving book *Bloodroot: Tracing the Untelling of Mother-loss* (Second Story Press, 2000), author Betsy Warland shares the very touching and tender journey of being present at the bedside of her dying mother. She paints a vivid picture of the kind of letting go required by our final release. She describes a moment where she gets a glimpse of other families' vigils.

"As I passed several patients' rooms, I noticed visiting family or friends often sitting with them in a strange, enervating silence. They sat apart. Rarely looking at one another. Staring inexplicably up at a corner in the room.

"When I returned to Mom's room, I looked up to see what was there. A television. Here, on their precarious edge, people watched television. As if this were intimacy. As if this was what was really happening."

Humans, it seems, are driven to distraction in the face of intimacy, particularly at times when we are in danger of entering deeper, potentially painful emotional territory. In coaching parlance, we call this uneasy space the "edge," as Warland intuitively does in her prose. It is a place where we start to get uncomfortable, and it is typically outside our comfort zones. Thinking and talking about death brings us to this edge and it is normal to engage in what are called "edge behaviors." Avoidance is chief among these. Acknowledging our mortality is painful. Naturally, we want to avoid pain.

There is another reason for our denial. The late Lou Tice, in his book *Personal Coaching for Results* (Thomas Nelson, 1997) opens with this: "Deeply rooted within our heart of hearts is the longing to grow and bloom, to express our creative, life-affirming innermost nature ... "

Later in his book, Tice goes on to describe human beings as teleological. Tice defines "teleological" saying, "We think in terms of purpose and we're naturally goal oriented. Having a teleological nature means that in order for us to change and grow, we need something tugging at us from the future, something to — quite literally — look forward to."

2. Talking about Death: A Social Shift

It is fair to say that no one, other than the very ill or desperate, looks forward to death. We are wired toward a kind of goal-oriented future optimism. So, it's natural that we have a hard time making sense of death. While there are some cultures that celebrate death — Mexico's Dia de los Muertos, for example, or the Hindu Pitra Paksha, or the Nepalese Gai Jatra — for most North Americans and Europeans the topic has become a kind of taboo. Even our vocabulary dances around the subject of death and dying, instead talking about passing away, crossing over, seeing the light, and other euphemisms. Talking about death is almost an anathema to us, given our natural tendencies to avoid pain (or painful subjects) and to look forward to the future.

Interestingly, there is a movement in North America, and one that is growing globally, to open up discussions about death. As Dr. Kathy Kortes-Miller wrote in her book *Talking About Death Won't Kill You*, (ECW Press, 2018), "Increased online exposure to death and dying gives us opportunities to learn about death from the virtual safety of our computers and digital devices. It brings conversations about illness and death out of the closet and into the light, acclimatizing us to the idea that death is part of life." The internet is helping with this, allowing those who wish to broaden the discussion the ability to connect in like-minded communities worldwide and have access to tools, resources, and guidance in dealing with delicate subject matter.

Take, for example, Death Cafes. The Death Cafe model was developed by the late Jon Underwood and Sue Barsky Reid, based on the ideas of Bernard Crettaz. Essentially, at a Death Cafe, people, often strangers, gather and eat cake, drink tea, and discuss death. The discussion is group-directed with no agenda or specific objective other than the nonprofit organization's stated purpose which is "to increase awareness of death with a view to helping people make the most of their (finite) lives." It is a social discussion rather than a grief support group or counseling session.

Death Cafes spread quickly across Europe, North America, and Australasia. According to the organization's website, deathcafe. com, there have been more than 6,500 Death Cafes in 56 countries since it launched in September, 2011.

Another example is Death Over Dinner. Death Over Dinner started with a University of Washington graduate course called Let's Have Dinner and Talk About Death, taught by Michael Hebb and Scott Macklin. It evolved into a website, deathoverdinner.org, and has become a global project. It launched in 2013 and in a single night tracked more than 500 dinners in 20 countries. Since then there have been more than 100,000 #deathdinners around the world.

The project provides a simple set of tools to help families and friends address the topic of mortality. Based on a collaboration between medical and wellness practitioners, the project brings together a wide array of individuals including oncologists, gravestone designers, palliative care experts, authors, curators, healthcare CEOs, and artists in a powerful movement to bring the conversation about death into mainstream culture.

Founded by mortician and author Caitlin Doughty, The Order of the Good Death "is a group of funeral industry professionals, academics, and artists exploring ways to prepare a death phobic culture for their inevitable mortality." Essentially, the Order supports a death-positive movement. Its mission, according to its website, "is about making death a part of your life. That means committing to staring down your death fears — whether it be your own death, the death of those you love, the pain of dying, the afterlife (or lack thereof), grief, corpses, bodily decomposition, or all of the above. Accepting that death itself is natural, but the death anxiety and terror of modern culture are not." The movement is growing with more than 100,000 followers on Facebook and members from across the world.

What these movements have in common is a reframing of how we view death. While recognizing our own mortality is difficult, to do so is not necessarily morbid. It gives us the opportunity to take stock, and to consider what really matters to us. Accepting our mortality means that we can more fully embrace our daily lives and it can act as a catalyst for us to think about what comes after, to consider what will remain after we are gone. It allows us to have a straightforward conversation with those we love or those responsible for executing our wishes after we are gone about what we want our legacies to be and how we want them implemented. Recognizing our own mortality is an essential part of creating your digital legacy plan.

In learning to accept mortality and overcome the taboo of talking about death, we may well look to the wisdom of the Dalai Lama. In his foreword to *The Tibetan Book of Living and Dying*, by Sogyal Rinpoche, His Holiness had this to say: "Death is a natural part of life, which we will all surely have to face sooner or later. To my mind there are two ways we can deal with it while we are alive. We can either choose to ignore it or we can confront the prospect of our own death and, by thinking clearly about it, try to minimize the suffering it can bring."

To quote the Death Cafe Facebook page, "Talking about sex won't get you pregnant and talking about death won't kill you." In fact, it may very well prepare you to face your own death, to act compassionately and competently on behalf of your loved ones, and relieve the anxiety and suffering of your children, heirs, or caregivers.

3. Seeking Spiritual Comfort Online and Offline

Depending on the reason you have purchased this book, you may find yourself in need of spiritual comfort as you progress through it.

It is possible you are an heir or executor, or the good friend or loved one of someone who has recently died. If you are crafting your own digital legacy plan, you will be contemplating your own mortality, as we discussed in the preceding section. This can be a tender place to be. Timing matters. Take on what you can, as you can.

Angela had the all too common experience of supporting her mother in hospice. Their days were filled with cups of tea, quiet conversation, art journaling, and the medical practicalities of her mom's care. It was an emotional time for them both as her mother had only recently retired. She was too young to die yet cancer decided otherwise. Suddenly, all of the end-of-life conversations had to happen in a rush without structure or planning.

After her mother's death, amid her grief, Angela fulfilled her duties as executor of the estate and dealt with myriad legal and practical details, as all executors must do. Along the way, she realized that she did not have the password to her mom's laptop, a tidbit of information that would surely turn up, eventually. Yet, it took nearly five years for Angela to find that password among dozens of personal files, many of which were an emotional trigger that renewed Angela's grief and slowed her progress through the records. Even with the password available, as of this writing, Angela hasn't had the courage to use the password to access the computer. It's a digital vault that might contain an emotional minefield. Angela wants to be prepared before she triggers that potential emotional explosion, an unintended side effect of her mom's digital legacy. This particular challenge of accessing digital information is unique to the twenty-first century. We are the first generations that have had to cope with it.

Later in the book we will discuss this and other aspects of dealing with death in the twenty-first century. The internet has changed us — not only in the dramatic ways we work and play, but also in the way we mark significant milestones such as weddings, anniversaries, births, deaths. Death, and the grief that goes with it, was once a very private experience. In the age of social media and the world wide web, death, like so much else, has become public.

Around the time we were drafting this book, world-renowned handbag designer Kate Spade and celebrity chef and writer Anthony Bourdain took their own lives within the same week. Most of us found out about this news via social media channels such as Facebook, Twitter, and Instagram. We amplified the news by posting it online for friends and followers to see. Around the world, people expressed their shock, sadness, and sympathy online. Through shared grief we sought comfort and understanding. Despite the sad circumstances of their deaths, they left behind legacies. Kate Spade's fashion aesthetic will influence generations to come. Anthony Bourdain has affected and changed the way the world views food and travel.

The decision to post, or not to post, about a death is a personal one. Much depends on the nature of the death and the renown of the person. For the families of Kate Spade and Anthony Bourdain, there was not much choice. Notoriety is often the cost of celebrity. For those of us who are not celebrities, we are faced with a choice and much will depend on our own preferences and those of our loved ones.

In late 2017, Vicki lost her beloved mother-in-law. She was 92 when she died and though she had started school in the days of the horse and sleigh, she had a computer and used email until very near the end of her life. While she had a healthy curiosity about just about everything, she never opened a social media account. Her private life remained private, as was the custom for most of her generation.

When Vicki and her husband received news of her passing, they instinctively sought comfort, first with each other and then as they notified more distant family and friends. The family chose the telephone, email, and snail-mail as methods of notification, as well as the printing of a traditional obituary in the newspapers.

Much of Vicki's daily life is typically played out openly online, setting an example with posting habits, being authentic, showing up in joy and sorrow, and sharing personal and professional insights and struggles. She feels it is important to advocate for good digital citizenship and positive social media. In this instance though, she chose to seek comfort in the world of touch and taste, what the digitally savvy call IRL — in real life. Partly this was out of respect for the privacy of her mother-in-law and the family and partly out of a desire to grieve privately.

In addition to cards, flowers, and offers of foodstuffs the family received many digital condolences via email, text, Instagram, and Facebook Messenger. They opted to forego a digital book of condolence as many of their mother's peers had predeceased her and those remaining were generally analog. Even though the digital options for notification and memorialization are numerous (we'll cover them in Chapter 7) this particular family chose a more traditional path for comfort and individual spiritual solace.

In a contrasting example, Carly (not her real name) began sharing the illness, treatment, and ultimate demise of her father very publicly in her Facebook feed. Part of her vigil involved ongoing trips from her small suburban town into the city where her father was hospitalized for treatment. She posted almost daily selfies of herself and her dear dad, and updates on the progress, or lack of progress, in his treatments. She shared details about her commute, the nursing staff, the family, and her ever-changing emotional states — the gamut of sadness, anger, gratitude, frustration, and fear.

Carly believes in God as a higher power, and she asked for prayers and strength as she navigated this very difficult terrain. Friends and followers responded generously to her posts, sharing their own stories, offering various devotions, and consoling her with words of encouragement. She sought, and received, comfort online.

Other examples of seeking comfort online are rampant on cultural milestones such as Father's Day or Mother's Day. Amid the thanks and congratulations to living relatives, it is common to see memorial posts as people use their social media accounts to acknowledge and grieve the passing of beloved family or friends.

More recently, with the outbreak of fentanyl-related drug overdoses and illicit use of pharmaceutical opioids rising globally, newsfeeds are rife with photos and stories of young people gone too soon, and pleas for action on the part of governments and health authorities.

Dealing with unexpected death, suicide, or the death of children is especially difficult. These kinds of deaths are more difficult to accept, and are often the subject of public discussion and debate. While the losses are deeply personal, their causes can become a part of a bigger conversation. It is important to be prepared for the amplification that can occur on social channels and in newsfeeds as the public seeks to make sense of things by offering solace, allocating blame, or engaging government agencies or officials.

In turn, government bodies see the challenges of social media's role in death. Angela had the unique experience of working with a governmental organization attempting to prevent aboriginal youth suicides. Sadly, teens in numerous remote first nations communities were using Facebook to make suicide pacts; a tragedy in the making if elders and frontline healthcare workers couldn't break the cycle. In order to do that, the adults had to quickly learn new digital life skills to navigate features, such as Facebook's Groups, to help the teens.

4. Tender Territory: The Importance of Self-care

Whether online or offline, or whether you are a churchgoer, or more secular in your belief systems, the need to find comfort and meaning in one of life's most common, and most assuredly certain events — death — is both human and natural. How you choose to find comfort is largely a matter of personal choice.

As you embark on digital legacy planning, we encourage you to practice self-care. You can start by mapping a self-care plan and crafting a contract to look after yourself. By knowing what comforts work for you, who to turn to, and having ready reminders of personalized supports, you'll support your own well-being. There's an example of a completed Self-care Contract in Sample 1. You can download a blank copy from the digital download kit included with this book. Print a copy and make some notes to document your Self-care Contract.

Many find that reading spiritual books or other literature can offer reassurance and consolation. Time spent in quiet contemplation or in nature can also help renew and nourish us. Let's not forget the basics: healthy food, sleep and rest, moderate exercise, and the circumspect use of alcohol or other drugs. You may find that keeping a journal is a helpful way to identify and process difficult emotions. Reach out to people you love and trust and let them know that you are dealing with legacy planning or estate management so that they can offer you support as needed.

Think about whether or not those you trust can be found online. Perhaps you belong to an especially supportive online Facebook group, or have streamlined your friends and followers lists so

Sample 1
Self-care Contract

<table>
<tr><td rowspan="12">**Self-care Contract**</td><td colspan="2">Date: January 16, 2019</td></tr>
<tr><td colspan="2">How do you know you are in the right frame of mind to undertake digital legacy planning or administration? Fill out this worksheet to assess your readiness and craft a plan to take care of yourself throughout the process.</td></tr>
<tr><td colspan="2">**Mark the response that suits your situation with 1 being poorly prepared and 5 being fully prepared.**</td></tr>
<tr><td>I am well rested.</td><td>☐ 1 ☐ 2 ☐ 3 ☒ 4 ☐ 5</td></tr>
<tr><td>I am well hydrated.</td><td>☐ 1 ☐ 2 ☐ 3 ☒ 4 ☐ 5</td></tr>
<tr><td>I have taken care of my physical needs such as exercise, meals, and fresh air.</td><td>☐ 1 ☐ 2 ☒ 3 ☐ 4 ☐ 5</td></tr>
<tr><td>I have a plan for taking breaks, and enlisting help if needed.</td><td>☐ 1 ☐ 2 ☐ 3 ☒ 4 ☐ 5</td></tr>
<tr><td>I have comfort items, either spiritual or personal, nearby.</td><td>☐ 1 ☒ 2 ☐ 3 ☐ 4 ☐ 5</td></tr>
<tr><td>A supportive person or trusted friend is aware of what I'm doing and is on standby should I need emotional support.</td><td>☐ 1 ☐ 2 ☐ 3 ☒ 4 ☐ 5</td></tr>
<tr><td>I have the time and space in my life to concentrate on these tasks without contributing to stress or overwhelm.</td><td>☐ 1 ☒ 2 ☐ 3 ☐ 4 ☐ 5</td></tr>
<tr><td>I have collected needed resources, checklists, passwords, and documents so my task will be easier.</td><td>☐ 1 ☐ 2 ☐ 3 ☒ 4 ☐ 5</td></tr>
<tr><td>I can give myself permission to stop or take a break if I feel overwhelmed, or need to process my emotions.</td><td>☐ 1 ☐ 2 ☐ 3 ☐ 4 ☒ 5</td></tr>
<tr><td colspan="3">**Use this section to remind yourself of the things that help you care for you.**</td></tr>
<tr><td></td><td>My favorite comfort beverage</td><td>Cup of tea</td></tr>
<tr><td></td><td>My favorite spiritual reading, music, or podcast</td><td>Vivaldi's *Four Seasons*</td></tr>
<tr><td></td><td>The name and number of my support person</td><td>Darlene
555-555-5555</td></tr>
</table>

The name and number of professional or technical resources I might need	Paul 556-556-5656
My favorite self-care activities are	running in the forest hot baths, candles
I will know I need to take a break when	I start fidgeting I get teary
Other	I need 7 hours of sleep

I agree to care for myself throughout the digital legacy planning process, using this self-care plan and the resources available to me, as needed.

_____ J. Smith _____

Sign here to make a contract with yourself.

that you can post more personal content to them specifically. You want to be prudent about with whom you choose to share your most personal information.

When it comes to death, to some extent, you can control when the news becomes public. For some, this will occur during the dying process while for others no announcement will be made until an offline mourning period is observed. Some deaths may never be announced digitally. Privacy itself *is* comforting. Having said that, the digital space is public. Not everyone wants anonymous condolences from strangers. Sometimes those strangers make the grief about themselves, not the mourners; a phenomenon known as "grief jacking." We talk more about the public and private nature of grief in Chapter 7: Online Memorial Planning.

How and when this most personal detail — the news of your death — is shared will be guided by your spiritual beliefs and cultural norms. If you've written a digital legacy plan, you can communicate your wishes about this to your family. The degree to which the deceased and their mourners have lived a digital life will also influence how much comfort is sought from the online community. In some cases, it will be appropriate to crowdsource practical support through services such as Meal Train (www.mealtrain.com), ride sharing, and other digital conveniences. Concurrently, you may also seek comfort from online condolence books and digital memorials, which we will talk about in Chapter 6. There may also be a need to start a crowdfunding campaign to fund treatments, comfort measures, or funeral costs. Oddly, social networks allow old-style community support to be reincarnated in digital form.

What is important here is that we understand the emotionally sensitive nature of the subject and ensure that we find the comfort or practical support we need. A big part of what we are undertaking as we deal with digital legacy planning is the simple human desire to keep some part of our dearly departed with us. We want to hold onto their wisdom, achievements, and life lessons, and we want to make sure that we honor their memory and their wishes.

Never before have we been able to store and access such an astonishing array of information about ourselves and our lives. It is possible, because of digital technology, to have an echo of ourselves in the world long after we are gone. This is the immortality promise of the internet.

5. Immortality Promise of the Internet

In her book *#Untrending: A Field Guide to Social Media That Matters* (First Choice Books, 2016), Vicki opens with a question: "What if every post you made was a forever post? A note from the now-you to the future-you; a message from present time cartwheeling out to the future and captured as your legacy — your leave-behind?"

She's asking you to consider the long-term implications of your social media posting habits, proposing, as she says later in the book that "everything falls victim to the eventual decay of its molecular structure, except perhaps the internet." If, in fact, the internet is here to stay, and there is every indication that it is, then your data is here to stay, too. That means every digital post, tweet, photo, document, or video could last a lifetime, or possibly several lifetimes. The internet, essentially, promises a certain kind of immortality. This may lead you to think more seriously about the messages and legacy you are leaving behind in permanent cyberspace. It also provides you with legacy options never before available.

A number of companies have entered the marketplace to offer services to help plan and secure digital immortality. Safe Beyond is a digital time capsule provider that allows you to create personalized future messages for your loved ones, promising easy access to all your digital assets and, they advertise, ensuring your legacy forever. Through the service you can leave date-based messages to be delivered on a special calendar date, such as a birthday or anniversary, or location-based messages that will be delivered when your loved one arrives at a specific geographic location.

Let's say you had always planned to visit the Eiffel Tower with a loved one. Sadly, the dream wasn't achieved in your lifetime. Using a time-capsule service, you can prerecord a message that your loved one can access once he or she arrives at the iconic location. Imagine event-based messages for future weddings, graduations, and, one supposes somewhat ironically, funerals. Final social media messages can also be part of the package. This kind of service allows us, effectively, to communicate with loved ones from beyond the grave, should we choose to do so.

Other similar services are cropping up. My Video Life Story (www.myvideolifestory.com/about-myvideolifestory.html) is the brainchild of Emmy award-winning documentary producer, Diane Hirsch. Her goal is to create entertaining and historical accounts that become priceless family heirlooms shared by family and friends to be relived over and over again. While tribute videos in and of themselves aren't new, My Video Life Story and other similar services are very much pitching the notion of a personal legacy that lives on in digital form long after we have physically passed on.

Eternime (eterni.me), a service that is currently in beta testing, boldly shouts on its website banner: "Who wants to live forever?" Offering to preserve your cherished memories, thoughts and stories, the proposed service goes on to suggest you could live life forever as a digital avatar. Eternime's algorithm will build a profile based on posts and interactions in your social media profiles and study your mannerisms and memories. This data would be used to create a digital you. Further, people in the future could actually interact with your memories, stories, and ideas, almost as if they were talking to you. The final tagline on the homepage reads "Become virtually immortal."

Lifenaut (www.lifenaut.com), based in Vermont, USA, offers participation in a long-term computer science research project that explores how technology may one day extend life through digital means. Bina48 is its ambassador, a social robot created using video interview transcripts, face recognition, laser scanning life mask technology, artificial intelligence, and voice recognition technologies. "She" interacts based on memories, beliefs, information, and values collected about one of Lifenaut's founders. Lifenaut is promoted as a safe space to store your life experience, offering users a free and offsite information back-up option for personality traits and other life lesson information that can be accessed in the future. It is an "organized and free personal digital archive ... created to help people build a rich profile of information that preserves their essential, unique qualities for future generations and family members."

This is new territory, and we are navigating a fine line as we stand at the crossroads of the analog and digital worlds. Current and yet-to-be-imagined technology provides ordinary mortals with opportunities to not only be remembered by future generations but also to potentially influence them. The same technology that powers Siri and Alexa, and the rapid advances being made in Artificial Intelligence (AI) put the possibility of an interactive, robotic, or holographic immortal version of ourselves well within practical reach.

In a sense, as Bell, Bailey, and Kennedy propose in their article in the journal *Mortality*, " ... the internet could be interpreted as a type of digital heaven where our loved ones continue their existence: a place from which they can reappear or be heard at any time, where the deceased become 'online angels'." (*Mortality*, 2015.)

Even with current technology, we are uniquely positioned to consciously choose how we want to be remembered, and for how long. While we are still living we can decide what kind of digital footprint we want to leave for posterity. For some, the idea of digital immortality is appealing. Others may find the idea disquieting, uncomfortable, or downright creepy. Many will prefer, as we discussed in the opening of this chapter, to avoid considering the issue at all. Some of you may even assume that eventually technical obsolescence, deterioration, or bit rot will take care of things. If only it were so.

6. Why You Can't Rely on Bit Rot

Bit rot is the slow deterioration in the performance and integrity of data collected on storage media. Digital files can spontaneously decompose, file formats become obsolete, and the applications used to read and access data are in a continual state of change. Data and information saved on removable media — think of the fate of floppy disks and cassette tapes — are problematic. There is no doubt that current technology and digital storage options will change, rendering present systems obsolete.

Nevertheless, relying on bit rot and technological degradation as a strategy to deal with your digital footprint is unreliable at best, and a very long-term play. Most hardware and software providers offer regular upgrades and updates to help keep present-day technology current. As an example, *PC Magazine* noted in a 2018 article, "the original .DOC file format created by Microsoft Word in the 1980s became a legacy format after the new .DOCX format debuted in 2007. Because billions of .DOC files exist in the world, Microsoft has continued to support the old format in all subsequent versions of Word, at least for now." Lesser-known products may not provide extended support, but in the short-term, you, your heirs, or loved ones will still have to deal with your share of the nearly 41.5 terabytes of data produced by the average US household, per year. Bit rot and technological change simply won't do the job.

The amount of data we produce is staggering, and deciding what to delete, store, or preserve after we are gone requires a thoughtful, systematic, and practical approach. In part, our decisions will be based on how we want to be remembered. This becomes a question of personal legacy.

2
What Is a Legacy?

In many ways, legacy is your message to the future. It's the echo of your current self across time. It's an amalgamation of the things you have done, said, and shared. Legacies, both positive and negative, live on as echoes after we die.

Before the internet, your legacy's echo would fade over time. Each successive generation would remember a little less about you and your contributions to culture, business, and society. At 102 years old, Angela's great grandfather died just as the internet was being invented. What remains of his story includes some war stories, memories of kindness and love, a few dozen photographs, and the recipe for his favorite treat, Christmas cake. Angela's generation is the last to have known him and when that generation is gone his echo will fade even further. Next century, who will remember this war hero who survived the horrors of both WWI and WWII and the life he lived over ten decades?

By contrast, with the internet, your echo has the potential to be perpetually amplified. Your stories live on in your own words through social media, your kindness and love are well documented, there could be tens of thousands of photographs of you, and your recipe collection is, in theory, eternally available on your blog.

Your digital legacy includes all these things and much more. The digital footprint that will become your digital legacy can be made up of a meaningful collection of wisdom and ideas, or an unremarkable addition to digital noise that can never be silenced.

What do you want people to remember about you? What impact do you want to have on the future? Some people won't care at all (and we're certain they haven't picked up this book), but many people will care (thank you, dear reader). Without due care and attention during your life, your digital legacy may not accurately reflect who you were and how you are remembered after death.

Historically, the reach of your legacy was limited by celebrity, inasmuch as leaders, politicians, and the notorious were known far and wide because of impact or reputation. Local farmers, homemakers, and one-room schoolhouse teachers left a legacy for their local community be that a small town, a farming village, or an entire county. By contrast, historical figures such as Cleopatra or Jack the Ripper were more widely known, but by no means global celebrities by today's standards. Even so, their legacies still have broad-reaching influence.

Today's celebrities have huge reach through the distribution of their movies, music, and musings via global distribution deals and social media. While most of us aren't household names like Angelina Jolie or Tom Cruise, we all have an element of celebrity in our digital footprint. When was the last time you Googled yourself? Take a moment to do it now. You may be surprised by how much or how little pops up about you, your work, and other aspects of your life.

Today, our reach isn't bound by geography nor is it constrained by the limitations of communication. In theory, anyone can have a global reach through social media, websites, and other online communities. Just as mass media has created opportunities for mass communication, digital media has limited reach only by the distance to the nearest internet café. This means that your digital legacy can reach an audience spread around the globe, a reality familiar to many after the extensive immigration of the last century.

With families and friends divided by geography and travel time, it's always taken effort to maintain relationships. As recently as the 1990s, long-distance phone calls were prohibitively expensive making real-time connections a luxury item for many families. Snail-mail letters were an economical alternative but they lacked immediacy as envelopes traveled the world courtesy of the US Postal Service, Canada Post, Royal Mail, and other post offices. In contrast, less than 30 years later, families today can keep in touch economically through video chat, text messaging, and social media. International phone calls are now free through WhatsApp. Facebook Live and Instagram Live videos make it possible to share moments in real time. How delightful for a grandparent in New Delhi to see their grandchild graduate from a Canadian university through livestreaming!

The global reach of accessible, real-time communication has made it substantially easier to foster community. Family and friends, artists and audiences, inventors and angel investors can all use today's communication tools to build community. In doing so, they gather a group of people, big or small, interested in their work, their contributions to society, across time through many generations. These are the people who care about your digital legacy in life and will nurture it after your death.

1. Legacy by the Generations

Over the last century, there's been a shift in the attention paid to legacy. What was vital to our great grandparents has different significance for younger generations. Each generation has been given a label for quick reference. Labels such as baby boomer and millennial are probably familiar while the dates and names of each cohort vary depending on the source. While there is no definitive breakdown, for this book the generations are defined as follows:

- Silent Generation, born 1920 to 1944

- Baby Boomers, born 1945 to 1964

- Generation X, or Baby Bust, born 1965 to 1976

- Millennials, or Generation Y, born 1977 to 1995

- Centennials, or Generation Z, born 1996 to today

Beyond date of birth, generations can also be defined by life experience. Those born on the cusp of a date range may self-select into an older or younger generation. For example, someone born in 1962 could consider themselves Generation X rather than a Baby Boomer. Keep in mind that membership in each generation can vary but, in broad terms, the following descriptions highlight the life experiences and digital exposure for each group.

Born between 1920 and 1944, the Silent Generation grew up in a pre-digital time. They were silenced as children in keeping with the child-rearing approach that children should be seen and not heard, typical of the early twentieth century. Later, they were further silenced as young adults under McCarthyism with fears that voicing their opinions would label them as Communist in the early years of the Cold War. They have lived through the creation of computers, space travel, and the birth of the internet. Some have eschewed digital life skills while others have embraced all things digital. This generation values history and sees their life work as leaving a legacy, digital or otherwise. Today's eldest citizens were born shortly after World War I. They grew up in the realities of the Roaring Twenties and the Depression in the 1930s. Family and country are priorities having grown up in the shadow of two world wars and the Depression. While some have embraced email and social media, the Silent Generation have lived much, if not all, of their lives without digital. Early photographs are treasured as they were rare and expensive luxuries. Communication is deliberate through letters, telegrams, and phone calls. For this generation, digital legacy is typically secondary as their words, likeness, wisdom, and experiences are shared by children, grandchildren, and great grandchildren. The Silent Generation has minimal interest and, possibly, limited understanding of their digital footprint.

Baby boomers, perhaps the most famous generation, were born between 1945 and 1964 in the wake of the prosperity following World War II. In those years, many wartime inventions became products for the home and office including computers, radio, ATMs, radar, and GPS. The space race to the moon brought technology into everyday imagination. As baby boomers entered the workforce and started their families, they contended with the issues of the civil rights movement and the quest for equal rights for women. A prosperous generation, they were among the first to purchase home computers, pagers, brick-like mobile phones, and cable television packages. Professionally, they lived the shift from manual typewriters to electronic keyboards and dot matrix printers. Some baby boomers embrace the digital life while others prefer to stick with analog ways. Baby boomers were also builders, and as a result, legacy — whether analog, digital, or bricks and mortar — can be important to them. Their personal digital legacies vary tremendously although most have had to adapt to digital professional legacies.

Generation X, born between 1965 and 1976, are those sandwiched between the larger baby boomer and millennial generations. This group is often credited with inventing the internet, Wi-Fi, online communities, social media, and more. They saw the potential in earlier technology, enhanced its function, and explored new ways to use it. Gen X are the generation that bridges the gap between analog and digital upbringings. They have been significant content contributors to the internet and are the first generation to have large digital footprints.

Millennials, or Generation Y, were born between 1977 and 1995. This was a transitional generation, where some remained analog while others, depending on access and inclination, quickly adopted emerging digital technologies. They grew up alongside the world wide web as it evolved from dial-up to high-speed. They have never known a world without electronic calculators, video games, and for some, internet research. They continually embrace new social media platforms, most recently Snapchat, perhaps to carve out their own online space away from older generations. This generation is often maligned for its desire for more flexible work-life arrangements but they are, in our opinion, pioneers of future standards for working conditions that use the best of technology to allow mobile workers to contribute at any time and any place. Like Gen X before them, they too have large digital footprints.

Today's children, born since 1996, are called Generation Z or Centennials. They have never known a world without the internet. Most have had access to computers and handheld devices from a young age. Some are getting specific guidance on how to use the technology responsibly while others are left to their own devices with their devices (pun intended!). This variability is creating a generation with hugely diverse digital life skills and their parents and teachers are writing the social norms around them in real time. This will be the first generation to be born and grow up in a fully digital world. Their digital legacies will be large combining both their own contributions and their parents' digital footprints. Many parents have shared multiple adorable baby photos, growing up milestones, and potentially embarrassing moments online. (Concurrently, there are a growing number of parents' who protect their children by not sharing their children's lives online.) This generation will also be the generation stewarding their parents' digital legacies in years to come.

While time is the common descriptor, historical events and shifts in technology can also identify generations. Those who experienced World War II have shared frames of reference with those who fought in the Gulf Wars. We also talk about digital immigrants and digital natives, with the former learning technology in adulthood shifting from broadcast television and newspapers to online news and streaming. Meanwhile, the digital natives have never known life without a tablet, Wi-Fi, and apps for every task.

2. How Digital Is Your Life?

When we look at digital legacies in the context of generations, it's helpful to consider a different lens, one developed by R "Ray" Wang in his book *Disrupting Digital Business: Create an Authentic Experience in the Peer-to-Peer Economy* (Harvard Business Review Press, 2015). Mr. Wang defines digital generations by the way they engage in technology. These include:

- "Digital natives" who have known digital all their lives and willingly embrace all digital opportunities at work and play.

- "Digital immigrants" who by choice or by requirement have transitioned from analog to digital.

- "Digital voyeurs" who are aware of digital and accept its existence but have not yet joined the digital ranks.

- "Digital holdouts" are those who are content with their non-digital existence and resist, even fear, any shift toward a more digital life.

- "Digitally disengaged" who have tried digital and have stopped using it. They are disillusioned by the broken promises of privacy, access, and so on.

When considering digital legacy, Wang's work is interesting because it empowers the individual to self-identify the digital life they lead regardless of chronological age. And each of the five types hints at the importance (or lack of importance) digital legacy holds for each user. In the absence of a digital legacy plan, generational clues may be all an executor has to work from to determine how to handle a digital legacy.

Whether you look at birthdates, self-identified digital generation labels, or some other marker to distinguish between users, digital use varies for every individual. It impacts how we interact with others online and offline and how we engage with topics from the mundane to the vital. For each person, legacy is different and the importance and urgency of digital legacy varies. It can also define an individual's sense of permanence in their social groups' consciousness after death. How permanent is that presence?

Common wisdom suggests legacy becomes more important as generations get older. As we reach middle age and begin to glimpse our own death on the horizon, does legacy become more important? More urgent? Maybe. Yet, maybe not. Does an increased sense of legacy correlate to age or to each generation? For the baby boomers, for example, the legacy of the bricks and mortar of a family home or business is legacy. In contrast, for example, the iterative digital legacies of Gen X's contributions to the internet are an intangible but equally lasting legacy. Or consider any woman's self-documentation in gender equality issues using the #metoo hashtag. Given the newness of digital legacies and digital living, we haven't yet got enough community experience with digital death to generalize everyone's experience based strictly on age. To guide your executor, take time to complete the Your Digital Life self-assessment worksheet (see Sample 2).

Taking the time to reflect on the importance of digital legacy can help you and your executor prepare for your eventual death.

3. Your Personal Legacy

Now, it's time to talk about you. What do you want people to remember about you? It may help to think of your digital legacy as a gift to your heirs and future generations. Your personal legacy, whether crafted or not, is a time capsule of your life, or as we

Sample 2
Your Digital Life Worksheet

Date: February 16, 2019	

Complete this worksheet to define your digital life and your digital values.

Age:	58
Gender:	Female
Marital status:	Married
Children:	2
Location:	Chicago
Other:	Presbyterian
What generation do you belong to?	Baby boomer
What is your approach to digital?	Digital immigrant
How much does legacy matter to you?	☐ 1 ☐ 2 ☒ 3 ☐ 4 ☐ 5 *It doesn't matter at all (1)* *It matters more than anything (5)*
How much of your digital legacy is important?	1 ☐ 2 ☒ 3 ☐ 4 ☐ 5 *None of it is important (1)* *Every file is vital (5)*
To what degree do you want to protect/preserve your digital legacy?	☐ 1 ☒ 2 ☐ 3 ☐ 4 ☐ 5 *Not at all (1)* *It must be protected completely (5)*
What do you want done with your digital assets?	☐ 1 ☒ 2 ☐ 3 ☐ 4 ☐ 5 *Delete all (1)* *Protect all (5)*

What percentage of your digital life is devoted to each of the following areas? Add notes, if desired to explain their importance.

Education	0%
Career	30%
Politics	0%
Economics	10% online banking side hustle
Shopping	10% Amazon, eBay

Fitness/Health	5% fitness tracker	
Religion/Spirituality	5% church newsletter	
Creativity	0%	
Home	0%	
History	0%	
Family/Relationships	30% doing this for my children	
Hobbies	10% glassblowing group	
Other		

discuss in Chapter 7, your "museum of me." Your family history, social and political opinions, personal experiences, and more, create an archive to preserve you. The details are a blend of the mundane, the everyday, and the deeply personal.

The mundane part of your legacy includes your mileage log, banking details, transit pass records, and grocery spending habits. It's the part of your digital footprint that is largely uncontrollable as you have no choice but to use online banking, swipe your transit card, or use your grocer's loyalty card. This data paints a picture of the life you lived, if it's accessible to future generations.

The everyday details in your personal legacy include the photos and videos you take, your social media posts, email correspondence, calendars, and so on. Your professional, artistic, or other digital work also falls under this category. It's the things you do as you go about your life. Small bits of data that accumulate to tell a story over a lifetime. You have the most control of your voice in this aspect of your personal legacy. You get to decide what images you capture, what you post, what you write, and more.

The deeply personal aspects of your life appear in your own data and elsewhere. Your doctor, for example, has detailed digital medical records that tell all your physical truths — pimples, vaccinations, broken bones, hemorrhoids, surgeries, dementia — the list grows with each year you live. Your therapist, counselor, coach, trainer, and others have similar personal data. Concurrently, you may be consciously creating deeply personal digital content through writing, photography, video, or other media. (Remember that digital content isn't always words on the screen.) Maybe you keep a gratitude journal, a digital diary, or have private chats with close friends through Facebook or WhatsApp. Maybe you and your spouse exchange sexy messages through text or email? The deeply personal aspects of your digital legacy can be deeply revealing, too.

You might choose to plan your digital legacy in an ad hoc way organizing specific parts of your life out of convenience. Alternatively, you might prioritize the elements of your digital legacy to review sexting with your spouse over emails with a colleague. Or you might take a systematic approach working logically from one part of your digital footprint to the next. It's also an option to ignore your digital legacy prior to reading this book and review how you use digital in your life from here forward being more mindful of what you create, what you post, and how.

It's important to remember that your personal digital legacy tells your story from your point of view. Even if you attempt to hide or delete certain information, there's a good chance that part of your story is recorded in someone else's digital legacy.

4. Legacy of Your Loved Ones

For generations, when a loved one dies, those left behind have had to navigate the material, emotional, and spiritual implications of the loss. Whether death was anticipated or unexpected, the things to consider are the same.

Part of our role is to steward our loved one's legacy. What did their social life, community interests, and professional work say about their values? How can that legacy best be honored? Are their elements that should remain private? Anything that should be destroyed? In Chapter 7, we offer some guidance about what to consider in curating your loved one's legacy.

5. Professional Legacies

In addition to their personal legacy, many people leave a professional legacy behind. Engineers contribute to buildings and bridges that are used for decades or even centuries. Musicians, artists, and writers leave expressions in sounds, images, and words that capture the world at a particular time and place.

The importance of your professional legacy may depend on your age or the kind of work you do. Some professional legacies are preserved digitally while many others only exist in real life. (IRL, remember?) A lifetime of work may have a few highlights that endure as legacy while the more repetitive day-to-day business tasks don't achieve legacy status.

In the survey we conducted with our digital peers, professional legacies were extremely important. There was explicit concern for anything that generates revenue. There was also a desire to preserve intellectual property; especially books and videos that reflect proprietary thought leadership. Yet, only 50 percent of this digitally savvy group have plans in place to secure their professional legacies after death.

The focus on the money aspects of a business's legacy may be too narrow a focus. A company's success is the sum of the entire operation. The equation to calculate that sum often includes intangible elements like the skill of a video editor, the charisma of the company's founder, or the interpersonal relationships of a few key staffers.

One reason for the lack of legacy planning is that some businesses are in the start-up phase or have reached a moment of exponential growth. Available resources are stretched thin as they focus on the tasks required to take advantage of every opportunity to grow the company. There is neither time nor energy to consider digital legacy planning. Even so, it's important to protect the infrastructure that supports revenue generation, as well as consider what parts of your work you want to live on after you are gone. These challenges are exacerbated if you are a small business or solopreneur.

Sylvia Taylor is a good example here. She is the author of two books, *The Fisher Queen* (Heritage House, 2012) and *Beckoned by The Sea* (Heritage House, 2017). In addition to her writing career, Sylvia offers consulting, coaching, teaching, and manuscript support to other writers. This has become a thriving small business. Her professional legacy will not only include her body of written work (published and unpublished) but also the intellectual property she has designed to complement her work in the form of workshop designs, vast quantities of research, speaking notes, and more than 400 published articles. Says Sylvia, "For me, the key word is 'legacy.' My body of work is not just how I make my living and pay my bills, but the gift I leave to the world in writing and publishing about such themes as ecology, female empowerment, cultural history, and so on."

Every professional needs to think about how their legacy lives on, whether from the financial or philosophical standpoint. Is your professional legacy ready for your death?

3
Assets and Access

Anyone who has reset a password knows the potential frustration of logging into any account online. Add in two-factor authentication and the frustration can grow, if, say, your account is verified with an old phone number.

Now, flash forward to a time after your death. How will your executor or family members access your digital accounts? They will need to know where to look for your digital information and how to access it.

Understanding your digital assets and appointing someone to steward them after your death are two separate but interrelated tasks. Only you know the full extent of your digital footprint. Creating a digital inventory will help your executor or family member find all your digital goodies, from PayPal funds to video collections. In this chapter, you'll explore your digital footprint and consider who will look after your digital legacy, whether that's your legal executor or a less-formal steward of your digital assets.

1. Digital Assets Inventory

To understand your digital assets inventory, you've got to think about all aspects of your digital footprint. For most people this is more than your Spotify playlists, online banking passwords, and social media accounts. To help you itemize your digital assets, we've developed a worksheet. Make notes as you read the rest of this section to create a detailed inventory. See Sample 3 for an example of the Digital Asset Inventory Worksheet. You can print out a blank copy from the download kit included with this book.

As you create your inventory, it's important to know that your data can be roughly organized into two categories: created and passive. You produce created data every time you take a photograph, write an email, or create a document. At the same time, common digital activities create passive data. You'll find this in your browser history, online shopping transactions, and streaming video recommendations lists. Some of your data will be accessible and familiar because you use it every day while other data may be hidden on your hard drive and thus forgotten.

Let's explore your digital assets.

1.1 Online banking

If you fill in just one part of your digital inventory, let it be about online banking. Your executor is going to need to know where to find your savings and your debt. While an appointment at the brick-and-mortar location with a copy of your last will and testament will give your executor access to your bank accounts, they may not be the only financial systems you're using. What if you have an overseas bank account or money saved in a bank that doesn't have physical locations? Your executor also needs to know if you have money on account with PayPal, Square, Etsy, or other online shopping environments where you might have credit. While not yet a regulated currency, you may hold one or more types of cryptocurrency. All of which add value to your estate and can be put to good use for your heirs.

If you own a business or run a side hustle, you may also have ongoing passive sales transactions or affiliate program income. Depending on the nature of your business, you may also have responsibilities through a payroll system, retirement or pension funds, tax

Sample 3
Digital Assets Inventory Worksheet

Digital Assets Inventory Worksheet		
	Date: March 16, 2019	
	Make notes on digital elements of your life to create an inventory of your digital assets.	
	Online banking	Bank of America
	Servers	none
	Websites	www.mybusiness.com
	Email and databases	me@gmail.com
	Storage solutions	Google Drive, Dropbox, iCloud
	Productivity services	Evernote
	Social media and online communities	Facebook, Linkedin, Facebook Group
	Shopping accounts	Amazon, eBay
	Internet access	high-speed internet/cellular data
	Loyalty programs and memberships	Wellness points, AIR MILES
	Gaming accounts	none
	Entertainment accounts	Netflix
	Events and tickets	Ticketmaster
	Medical attention	travel medical insurance
	Academic interfaces	none
	Other	none

withholdings, sales tax, and more. Help your executor find your money by listing all your online banking accounts and obligations on the inventory.

1.2 Internet access

Getting online is a vital access point for all digital citizens. You may connect at home or the office or both. You might also add a mobile connection with a data package on your cellular phone service. Add to that public internet access points at the local library, retailers, commuter train stations, and other public places. How and where you access the internet adds to your digital footprint with server names, passwords, and related data. Your executor needs to know where you access the internet so that they can have your estate pay for ongoing internet service, if needed, or to cancel the service so your estate doesn't incur the expense after you die.

1.3 Servers

Next, add servers to your digital inventory. These mega computers can be used for data storage, email management, and as a portal to get you on the internet. Your family may have a media server, too, to house your digital music, movies, television shows, and home video. In some cases, the servers that are part of your digital life are managed by someone else and, in other cases, the responsibility falls to you and, when you die, your executor. Your executor needs to know what servers to look for after your death. Some servers will be maintained as part of your digital legacy while others will be decommissioned, per your wishes.

1.4 Websites

Do you run a website personally or professionally? Add all your websites to your digital inventory. For now, just list the URL. Later, you'll add details such as the login and password to get into the dashboard or back end of each website. When Angela completed her digital inventory she had to add her main self-hosted website used for professional purposes as well as a dozen domain names reserved for future projects. In addition, she included the two Wordpress.com sites where she blogs for fun. Angela's list also includes a few websites owned by others where she has contributed content. The websites listed on your digital inventory may be complex like Angela's list or you may have no websites at all. Either way, that's important information for your executor to have so he or she can manage your digital legacy effectively. The person will have to take charge of the domain registry, web hosting, related subscription services, e-commerce functions, and the content on each site.

If you have any doubt that the internet never forgets, have a look at your site (or someone else's) on the Wayback Machine; a web service that archives snapshots of websites on various days. The snapshots are taken by bots that capture what they see on the day of the visit. Try it at archive.org/web.

1.5 Email and databases

If you have a digital life, you've got at least one email address to note on your digital assets inventory. Pause to consider all your email addresses: Do you have one for personal use, another for work, and, maybe, a third for school? Email can be a critical access point for your executor to get at your digital assets so be sure to empower them with a complete list. The email address, password, and login access URL will all be useful. If you have more than one email address, make note of your primary address or explain for your executor how you use each address so that he or she can prioritize correspondence over shopping coupons. You might also note if you have one or more folders of email that you want deleted upon your death. Understandably, you won't want your heirs reading your not-safe-for-work (NSFW) notes to your spouse.

Make note, as well, if you use email as a marketing tool. Your executor or steward will need access to your email list service and/or the email functions in your customer relationship management (CRM) software. Empower your executor to know if you use a service such as Constant Contact, MailChimp, Infusionsoft, or Outreach Plus.

1.6 Storage solutions

Where do you keep your digital information? You'll probably find a lot of your data on servers, computer hard drives, and mobile phone memory chips. If you're using a cloud-based storage system, you'll have data on iCloud, DropBox, Google Drive, or all three! Add to that technology that you don't use any more such as old phones and laptops. In addition, some information may be on SD cards, USB drives, external hard drives, CDs, DVDs, or floppy disks. Ideally, you'll declutter your data before you die but it is important to make note of all your current storage solutions, no matter how messy so that your executor knows to look for them. You could also prioritize the data so that your steward knows the old college essays on floppy disks are less important than the family photos in Dropbox, for example.

1.7 Productivity services

Are you a busy parent or business owner? Or both? If you've got multiple calendars to manage and numerous concurrent projects on the go, then you are likely using a variety of productivity services for communication and time management.

Beyond email, are you using an instant messenger account such as Facebook Messenger or a team communication tool such as Slack? What about your digital calendar? Make note if you are using iCal, Outlook, Google Calendar, or another calendar app. If your executor has access to your calendar, it will be easier for him or her to cancel any posthumous appointments, recurring payments, or other details that you've recorded on your calendar. The person may also be able to glean some family or professional history if you've scheduled annual appointments or reminders for birthdays and anniversaries.

1.8 Social media and online communities

For some, social media will be a huge category listing dozens of online communities where you have relationships, contribute content, and interact with others. If you don't use social media, quickly note that on your inventory and move onto the next section. Similarly, if you don't care what happens to the social media accounts you use, then add that to your notes on the inventory so your executor knows. However, if you use social media or participate in other online communities, start making a list for your executor now. Don't forget to include both the accounts you use personally and those that you use professionally.

Your list should include every account whether you use it or not. Frequently used accounts on familiar social media sites such as Facebook, YouTube, Instagram, LinkedIn, and Twitter will be easy to remember. You'll also know if you're participating in social networking sites that are more common in other countries or feature a non-English language as the default. Examples include VK (Russia), RenRen (China), and Orkut (Brazil). Take an extra moment to recall if you have accounts on less-used social media sites. Maybe you have a Twitter account but haven't tweeted since 2009? You may wish to close such unused accounts now, to save some steps for your executor later. Your list should also include specialty sites such as 500PX, a photography community, or Ravelry, for knitters and crocheters. For now you'll list where you have accounts. As you make more thorough notes for your executor, you'll add usernames and passwords (or the password for your password manager — see Chapter 5).

1.9 Shopping accounts

Your executor needs to know where you shop online. If you do all your shopping in person, note this for your executor and move onto the next section. However, if you do buy things online, you'll know the vast amount of information that can be found in your wish lists, shopping carts, order history, and payment records. In part, your executor needs to know where you shop so he or she can secure any stored credit card information. This should include your PayPal, Square, cryptocurrency, or other online payment solution. The person also needs to know so he or she can ensure delivery of goods you ordered before you died, and access returns or warranties on goods that were delivered to you.

Your online shopping will likely encompass physical goods and virtual goods. Physical goods can range from books and clothes to food and housewares plus big ticket items such as home electronics, vehicle parts, and more. If you have movies, television shows, books, and games on iTunes, Google Play, or other vendors, you may have a substantial virtual library. However, like so many digital things, you may not be able to guarantee your media library will be available to your heirs.

Both iTunes and Google Play make their Terms of Service readily available to users. The documents are mostly written in everyday language rather than legal terms so they are easy to understand. What's clear for both companies is that the content is purchased by you and that you don't have authority to distribute it to a third party. iTunes notes, "When a Family member leaves or is removed from the Family, the remaining Family members may no longer be able to access the former member's Content." Google Play's terms as of October, 2018, tell us that "After completing a transaction or paying the applicable fees for Content, you will have the non-exclusive right, solely as expressly permitted in these Terms and associated policies, to store, access, view, use, and display copies of the applicable Content on your Devices or as otherwise authorized as part of the Service for your personal, non-commercial use only." Personal use, hmm. So, does that mean the media library dies with you? Maybe. Maybe not.

Much of the content — books, music, movies, television — can be downloaded and you may keep a copy for personal use on your own media server. So, you could download your entire iTunes or Google Play library and bequeath the server to your loved ones. If you have a large video library, this would require a huge storage disk and an investment of time to manage the downloads. However, streaming is more common today so that content is consumed in real time from Apple or Google's servers. In order for your family to continue to consume the content, the owner's account must be active. In theory, that account can be maintained, as long as the log-in email and password are known and a valid payment method is available. Neither company explicitly states what will happen to your access to purchased content after you die. Accessibility to stream your content after death is, at this point, a murky area in your digital legacy.

For the latest on iTunes Terms of Service visit
    www.apple.com/legal/internet-services/itunes/ca/terms.html.

To read Google Play's current Terms of Service visit
    https://play.google.com/intl/en-us_us/about/play-terms.html.

You may also shop for services online. Do you have an account with Uber or Airbnb? Have you set up your Starbucks card or public transit card to auto reload at specific intervals? Do you have any money on file in your account at your favorite spa, restaurant, or car detailing place?

In Chapter 6, we talk about the vast number of online accounts in common use. You may be surprised at how quickly your inventory grows.

1.10 Loyalty programs and memberships

Ah, loyalty programs! It is so much fun to get the perks offered by Starbucks or AIR MILES. If you've been hoarding your rewards, then there will be some perks leftover for your heirs, if the terms of service allow you to bequeath those benefits. Depending on the size of your estate, these may be welcome treats. Beyond any remaining perks, your executor needs to know about your loyalty programs so your accounts can be closed.

Concurrently, your memberships need attention when you die. Do you belong to a gym, professional association, Toastmasters, or a buying club? Your executor needs to know so he or she can cancel your membership and stop any monthly or annual payments. If you've built relationships within any of these organizations, the executor may also want to post, distribute, or publish your obituary or digital memorial to inform fellow members of your death. You'll read more about social media obituaries in Chapter 6.

1.11 Gaming accounts

Your digital inventory should also include your online gaming. You might participate in government-sanctioned gambling, have subscriptions on aggregate gaming services such as STEAM, or individual accounts with Minecraft, World of Warcraft, or myriad other games. In addition, you may have mobile phone game apps. If you don't do any online gaming, make a note and skip ahead to section 1.12.

At first glance, you may wonder about the value of listing your gaming accounts. In most cases, the value of the in-game goods or services have limited value in real life. However, your executor can help your in-game friends, associates, and game masters by notifying them of your death. If you've played a game such as World of Warcraft for years, your in-game friends will grieve for your avatar. This is a new and interesting element for obituaries and death notices. We'll talk more about this in Chapter 7. Help your executor by noting not just the games you play but your in-game personas, as well.

1.12 Entertainment accounts

Digital living has changed the way we consume entertainment. Whether you like movies or music, television series or books, you can stream or download a great many amusements. While you're creating a digital inventory make notes of all the services you use. Do you pay for access to programming on Netflix, Hulu, Prime Video, CBS All Access, Crave, or other services so you can watch television and movies? Add your book and magazine sources, too whether you subscribe to services such as Kindle Unlimited and Texture; borrow library ebooks through apps such as Overdrive; or purchase your reading material on iBooks or Google Books. Also include your music collection whether you curate playlists on Spotify or Apple Music or purchase songs and albums on iTunes or Google Play. Your executor or steward needs to know where to look for the content you've paid for and arrange to pass it on to your heirs, if the service permits, and to stop payment on auto-renewing subscriptions.

1.13 Events and tickets

Ticketed events can add to your digital legacy. If you're a sports fan, you may have waited years to get your family's season tickets for the local NHL, NBA, or NFL team. Similarly, performing arts fans may have season tickets to the theater, ballet, opera, or symphony. Add to that one-off events such as inspirational speakers, stadium concerts, and other one-time events. Your executor or steward needs to know what events you attend so he or she can secure your tickets, pass them on to your heirs, and designate new primary contacts for your long-awaited season tickets. It is also helpful to note on your digital inventory any ticketing services you use such as Ticketmaster or Eventbrite.

1.14 Medical attention

While access and costs for medical services vary by country, patients in any medical system often have to be the communication link between community health clinics, family doctors, pharmacists, specialists, technicians, and surgeons. To facilitate that communication, your digital footprint includes various test results, diagnosis, prescriptions, recommendations, and other details. Your healthcare practitioners are responsible for the privacy and security of the medical or health files in their care, even in the event of their retirement, incapacity, or death. In turn, any digital copies you have in your personal files are your responsibility and will make up part of your digital legacy. You may want to instruct your executor to delete all your medical records or, alternatively, instruct the person to keep the records for your genetic heirs' reference. The latter is especially valuable if your family lives with hereditary illness. Even simple things, such as telling your daughter the age when you entered menopause, for example, can be a helpful guide for her health in future.

In addition to your medical records, your digital footprint might include video chat conversations with a healthcare provider; travel medical documents; health insurance correspondence; or logins for blood clinics and other services where you can access results online. Ideally, your executor will have sufficient information to secure your accounts and close them, as appropriate. It is particularly important that your personal health or services card number (where applicable) and insurance account numbers be reported as deceased to prevent fraudulent use of your identity to access health services.

1.15 Academic interfaces

You will need to find and identify your academic information to empower your executor to secure your digital legacy. Each school you attended will have some digital records about you. Most importantly, your digital records in each school system are attached to a student identification number. Empower your executor with this number for each school you attended so that he or she can, if necessary, report your death to the school to prevent fraudulent use of your credentials.

If you are currently a student, you'll likely have an email account issued by the school as well as a variety of academic records such as your transcripts and standardized tests plus emergency contact details, health records, and disciplinary actions. Postsecondary students often have access to a digital learning environment that supplements online and in person courses through platforms such as Canvas, Moodle, or Desire to Learn (D2L). Lifelong learners may access these systems or other online education platforms such as Thinkific or Webinar Jam. Whatever platforms you are actively using at the time of your death, can help your digital steward identify the instructors and administrators who must be informed of your death.

From internet access to email to gaming to academics, your digital footprint has the potential to stretch in many directions at once. The bigger your digital footprint, the bigger the job it is to steward your digital legacy. In life, you can work to declutter your data and simplify your digital footprint. In death, you can support your executor by leaving clear information about the scope of your digital footprint. Remember that the Digital Footprint Worksheet is a guide. You should feel empowered to add any elements of your digital life that fall outside the common categories described in this section.

2. Who Has Control? Who Has Access?

When it comes to control of your digital footprint, there's a lot of information to share that identifies where your digital legacy can be found. Many elements will become the responsibility of the executor named in your will, if you have one. You should have one no matter your age! This executor will have legal authority over anything money related: banking, credit cards, PayPal accounts, and so on.

Your executor may also take control of your other digital assets; your intellectual property, websites, social media profiles, and so on. However, these can also be managed by a steward who understands your digital life. This might be your spouse, your business partner, your virtual assistant, or any other trusted person with the digital savvy to secure your digital legacy. In many cases, your executor and your steward may be the same person. In other cases, two or more people will take on these roles.

If you want a say in who takes control and what they do with your digital legacy, you need to complete your digital legacy plan (keep reading to keep creating it) and communicate your wishes to those people. While written instructions are helpful, it is best to share written instructions with your executor and your steward while you are still alive so that they can ask clarifying questions about your intentions and wishes. If that's not possible, you'll have to trust in their judgment to interpret your wishes and act on them accordingly.

3. Legal Mechanisms

Legalities around digital assets are evolving in response to the increasing amount of data and technology in our lives. The governing laws vary by jurisdiction although there are recurring themes in many places. In some cases, federal statutes are in place but the regional (state, provincial) laws have not yet been written. In other cases, older laws set out in the 1980s, at the dawn of the world wide web, are in place and need amendments to reflect today's internet. It's an evolving legal ecosystem that's doing its best to keep up with the fast pace of technological change.

Legally, if you die with a last will and testament in place, the executor you appoint in your will can take control of your affairs when you die. If you die without appointing an executor, the courts may let the public trustee (where one exists) do the job, unless someone comes forward, such as your next of kin, and applies and is approved to be the administrator of your estate. All of the rules around probate can vary by state, province, or territory.

Whether selected by you or by the court, the executor has clear authority over tangible items such as your money, possessions, and property. Your executor's legal status in regards to your digital footprint is murkier. The notion of digital ownership is murky because the terms of service for many online accounts don't state what happens to your information when you die. Beyond the legality of bequest, both tangible and digital, there are additional layers of complexity for protecting revenue, intellectual property, creative assets, privacy, and unfinished work. The digital age is certainly a complex time; one that will flex and challenge existing laws and require new laws to address twenty-first century issues.

Digital savviness is one issue that all executors face. The person you appoint may be a technical wizard familiar with online banking, social media, content creation and more. However, it's just as likely that your executor does not have these digital life skills. If this is the case, it is helpful to appoint a digital steward to work with your executor. Legacy contact, digital executor, and technical advisor are all alternate names for this relatively new role. In this book we use "digital steward" to indicate the person who will oversee your digital legacy.

A book such as this one cannot fully represent laws nor interpret legal precedents and proceedings as they relate, in this case, to digital assets. However, we can provide an overview of key issues and links to authoritative legal sources for more information.

In the USA, the American Bar Association has published a brief ebook by lawyer Michael D. Walker. His writing helpfully summarizes the legal complexities and flux around digital assets in the United States. Mr. Walker highlights the interplay of the Stored Communications Act (SCA) and Computer Fraud and Abuse Act (CFAA) with the more recent Revised Uniform Fiduciary Access to Digital Assets Act (RUFADAA). Add to that the implications of the Electronic Communications Privacy Act (ECPA) and the related revisions in The USA Patriot Act (USA PATRIOT). Just the initialisms can give you a headache! Similar complexities of overlapping and evolving laws are echoed in other countries' legislation and legal precedents.

If you'd like to read more, Michael D. Walker's ebook and other resources are available at www.americanbar.org. Search for "digital assets" and related terms to find relevant materials.

One of the key elements legally is to determine which digital assets have economic value and which have no economic value. Anything that can be translated to currency in the real world will need to be handled by your executor. This might include online banking, cryptocurrency, PayPal or Square balances, affiliate income, and more.

Next, it's helpful to understand if legal proceedings distinguish between files stored on your local device (mobile phone or computer) and files stored on remote servers or in cloud storage systems. In general, all files are considered to be your property to some extent.

Accessing files can be a challenge. Much of the law around digital assets is concerned with protecting privacy and we can all be thankful for that protection in the information age. However, after death, it can be a challenge for your executor or steward to gain access to your information. If the person knows where to look (referring to your digital assets inventory, ideally), the service provider might be able to provide non-content information. This could mean a list of the file names, email subject lines, or Facebook groups you manage. However, the authority may not stretch to include the content within your files. Think of it as getting a digital present where you can only look at the gift tag, not the gift in the box. If you have prepared a digital legacy plan in consultation with your lawyer or notary, you can explicitly grant access to your files so that your executor or steward can see them.

In Chapter 6, we'll give you some suggestions for ways to secure your social media and other accounts. In brief, Facebook's Legacy Contact is a good example. By setting this contact in your Facebook profile, you are informing Facebook of your consent to allow the person named to see within your profile when you die. As you'll read, not all services offer this level of decision making. As such, adding a legal letter of permission to your digital legacy plan may allow access. A lawyer or notary can best inform you of available options in your jurisdiction.

In Canada, the Osgoode Hall Law School at York University has published a particularly helpful resource written by lawyer Ian Hull (blog.osgoodepd.ca/digital-assets-planning-incapacity). This article summarizes the distinction between digital assets and digital accounts. Digital assets are files such as a photograph or text controlled by the individual. In contrast, digital accounts are online services such as Facebook that provide access to a service. In Canadian law, digital accounts are further refined into three categories: accounts that include "actual currency," "virtual property," and "personal or commercial information." While these definitions are understood in Canada, provincial laws have not yet been updated to reflect them. "As a result, if a party does not include a specific designation regarding digital asset management in their power of attorney, their legal representatives may find themselves restricted from accessing and managing these digital assets or accounts by a service provider's privacy rules, or their terms of use." This highlights, once again, the importance of a digital legacy plan.

Lawmakers around the world are having to explore and respond to the issues of digital assets and digital bequests. Although laws may seem unchangeable, they are not a fixed thing. As lawyers present arguments to the courts, laws are being interpreted in new ways every day. When it comes to digital information, society is writing new laws and rewriting existing ones to suit new circumstances. It's an iterative process. One that requires discussion, debate, and compromise. This is an evolving area of law as our lives become increasingly digital. If we want a say in who can access our data after we die, we need to be proactive in life and discuss the legal mechanisms with both a lawyer and our heirs.

4
Legacy Planning Options

An effective digital legacy plan provides specific guidance to your executor or steward. While you can make granular decisions for each individual element of your digital footprint, it will help your planning process and ensure a coherent digital legacy plan if you are clear on the legacy planning options available to you. In this section, you'll read about four common scenarios.

1. Make Your Choice before Death

Do you want to be a "digital zombie"? Researcher Debra J. Bassett coined this term to identify the deceased who continue to live through social media and other technology. ("Who Wants to Live Forever? Living, Dying and Grieving in Our Digital Society," *Social Sciences*, 2015.)

Whether you want to or not, it is entirely possible that a digital zombie is what you will become if you fail to take matters in hand while you are still living. As part of our research for this book, we surveyed a cross-section of our peers. They range in age and demographic attributes. Most have made a significant investment in the digital space, either because they do business, offer digital expertise, or create content that is crafted, distributed, or stored online. Nearly all have incomplete or nonexistent digital legacy plans, despite their level of investment in the space.

Some are highly motivated to preserve their digital footprints for financial or other reasons, others understand that it might be disturbing for their loved ones to stumble across them in cyberspace after they have departed. Many haven't really thought about it.

Megan Fox, a voiceover artist and copywriter, said one of her priorities would be "to close down all social media accounts because it can be so hard to see the face of a loved one that's no longer there." Megan is getting at the heart of what it means to allow yourself to become a digital zombie. She hopes to create and produce a plan that will phase her out of digital life, leaving behind only certain things she approves of in advance.

One thing our peers agreed on: It is important to start thinking about these choices before death. The only way Megan can have the kind of control she hopes to have and prevent the emotional hardship she alludes to for her loved ones is by making those choices now.

2. Death by Unnatural Causes

As difficult as it may be to talk or to think about, the nature of your death may in and of itself contribute to how you are remembered. Especially difficult is death by suicide. In addition to all the expected emotions that loved ones feel upon the loss of someone they care about, suicide complicates matters. Very often those that are left behind are angry, confused, or simply in shock. They may be tempted to erase all record of your life before death as a reaction to their very strong feelings, or to simply ignore the digital aspects of your legacy in response to their shock.

In their article in *Mortality*, Jo Bell, Louis Bailey, and David Kennedy talk about the mourning process following suicide in this way: "The mourning process following a suicide is more complex and difficult than for other types of death. The specific features that make suicide bereavement different to other types of death include the thematic content of the grief, which can often leave the bereaved confused, angry and burdened with guilt. Wider social reactions and processes serve to further stigmatize and isolate the bereaved. People may experience less social support because others may be unsure of what to say or how to respond to the death or may actively distance themselves from the bereaved." ("We do it to keep him alive: bereaved individuals' experiences of online suicide memorials and continuing bonds," *Mortality*, 2015.)

Particularly in the case of young people, who are the most likely to have a large digital footprint, death by suicide can become the subject for the grief itself. In many cases the dead person becomes an icon or rallying point for a movement to prevent further tragedies. If you, or someone you know may be considering taking their own life, please reach out to the appropriate resource in your town or region. Nearly all cities in every country offer suicide prevention services.

What about violent death? If you die while engaged in criminal activities, domestic abuse situations, or in rising incidences of public terrorism, your life and death will be in part defined by your demise. These circumstances present unique challenges to digital legacy planning.

Sudden death from misadventure, accident, or unanticipated illness can also create chaos for a family and for those managing the estate. The more you can do now to dictate the terms of your own legacy, the better it will be for those left behind.

While we may all wish to die peacefully from natural causes, surrounded by loved ones after having lived a full and rich life, that simply may not be the case. This only serves to emphasize why preparation is key, and thinking carefully and thoughtfully about your personal legacy and what you want it to be can make all the difference.

3. Bequeath Your Digital Life

Unlike your tangible property, the distribution of your digital assets is less defined. For example, your mother can bequeath a diamond ring to you and once you take possession of the ring your ownership of the inherited property is clearly in place. It's quite different again, if your mother wants to bequeath her recorded videos on YouTube to you. As they are housed in a digital space, you won't take physical possession of them. As Jed R. Brubaker et. al noted, "inheritance as a model often presumes a defined heir, which is not necessarily the case with online accounts and data." ("Stewarding a Legacy: Responsibilities and Relationships in the Management of Post-mortem Data," CHI, 2014.)

Ideally, you will bequeath your digital assets to a digital-savvy person who can then ensure your various accounts end up dealt with according to your wishes. In practice, you're not bequeathing digital assets so much as appointing a steward to look after your digital interests after you die. In Chapters 5 and 6, we'll cover how to appoint a digital steward and detail the ways you can pass on social and digital accounts. You will be entrusting this person to ensure your wishes are followed and to help identify, for your less digitally savvy family and friends, the important aspects of your digital legacy wishes.

There may also may be digital assets that have a distinct value in actual dollars. Do you have points programs attached to credit cards, hotels, or airlines? Your entertainment library (music, books, movies, or games), as mentioned in Chapter 3 can represent thousands of dollars in downloaded content.

Our friend Fred, mentioned in the Introduction, has a vast online collection of music and films. He wants to make sure his son has access to it after he dies. It not only represents thousands of dollars but many hours of curation. Fred has backed up his collection on a monster-sized hard drive and has shared the passwords to the archive with his son.

If you have digital revenue sources from YouTube, online courses, Patreon accounts, or book or product sales, you will want to note these as part of your estate planning. If you are an online influencer, it means you have invested a great deal of time and sweat equity in amassing online fans and followers and building a community of trust. How do you want that community served after your death? Who will act as a community manager on your behalf, either to sustain the community or to phase it out?

Shirley Weir, a colleague of ours, decided a couple of years ago to open up the conversation about menopause. She now has a thriving online community on Facebook of more than 7,000 people, and growing. She is the author of *Mokita: How to Navigate Perimenopause with Confidence and Ease* (Influence Publishing, 2018), and hosts a nationwide forum of the same name. Shirley is definitely a rising social influencer. She is bringing a much-needed conversation to the forefront and reaping the benefits and rewards of being first past the post on this important issue.

As yet, Shirley has not considered a legacy plan for her work. She knows how important it is in the world, and is being widely recognized in media and the community as a pioneer in this area. Her start-up has been rapid. Who will look after Shirley's community should something happen to her? How will her assets, both analog and digital, be preserved and transitioned?

In another example, Vicki, as an extension of her coaching practice, hosts an online Facebook group called the Big Fat Yes Club. It is a small but thriving online community, devoted to support and inspiration for doing business with integrity, from a place of personal alignment. On behalf of the membership-based Big Fat Yes Club, Vicki produces a quarterly magazine called *Pause: A tiny magazine that doesn't hustle, boss, crush, or slay* as well as maintains a database and a monthly newsletter.

Together with colleagues like Angela, Vicki produces content for the community as well. Should the community survive Vicki? To safeguard the community, and her Facebook assets, Vicki has named a digital legacy contact on Facebook, and provided shared group administrative access to her business assistant, as well as a couple of trusted social media associates. If the community is to continue and thrive, for itself, or as a legacy, it will need to be managed and moderated effectively.

Comanaged Facebook groups, such as Social Media Mindfully, and Death in the Digital Age, that Angela and Vicki share, are safeguarded by virtue of having partners sharing access, administration, and decision-making abilities. Whether your online community is large or small, it bears thinking about and planning for.

If you are an artist, photographer, writer, or creating useful digital content, your body of work can live on after you are gone. You need to decide how much, or how little will continue and who will manage it for you.

Cynthia Lockrey, a public relations and patient advocacy expert and the author of two books, *Your Child's Voice* (Self-Counsel Press, 2018) and *Bed Rest Mom* (Self-Counsel Press, 2018) had this to say: "I've worked hard to create a number of digital products and blog posts to help people share their stories and have their voices heard. I would love to see the blog posts on my website live on. I care less about my personal footprint and more about the professional footprint."

She goes on to say, "We spend so much time creating content but I expect many of us do not stop [to] think about [what] will happen to that content after we are gone. It would be a shame if all that hard work just disappeared. Some people may prefer their digital work to leave when they leave, as it relates directly to them. Whereas others, like me, would love for people to continue to get help and support through our volume of digital work."

Cynthia clearly wants her wisdom and advocacy to be an ongoing legacy to the community she serves. Making a plan to secure that future for her work is an important step.

What about unpublished intellectual property? Should you be a rising star in your field like Shirley, or someone who has already developed any level of celebrity for your work, there will be those who will be interested in what you have not yet completed. How do you want to handle that? Leaving clear instructions in the hands of your estate planner, or your digital legacy steward will help.

What about hardware assets, such as expensive smartphones, laptops, tablets, desktop computers, and the associated gadgetry? There may be people in your life who would appreciate these assets. These devices may be an integral part of how your home or business functions. Consider how you bequeath these devices. Most legal wills don't deal with small personal items such as electronics, jewelry, artwork, or personal collections, unless they have a significant dollar value. You can add your hardware or gadgetry to a personal bequest list, much as you would for other treasured personal items.

4. You're up for Digital Adoption

If your estate documents don't include a digital legacy plan in some form, your digital life is up for adoption. The executor of your last will and testament will have authority over digital assets that have value; online banking, mortgages and other debt, digital money balances on PayPal and Square. How digitally savvy is your executor? Would the person know to check your PayPal balance?

Beyond the money stuff, your executor may not know much about your digital life. If so, your social media profiles and other digital assets are up for adoption IF you have a friend or family member who wants to take responsibility for your digital legacy. In the absence of instructions from you, that person will make his or her own judgments about what to do and not do with your profiles, content, and other elements of your digital footprint. Of course, even a digitally savvy steward might not find all your digital secrets. Even if the person can find some, he or she may not be able to gain access based on the terms of service for each service.

Even with incomplete access, if a digital steward steps forward to adopt your digital footprint, your digital legacy will be deleted, curated, and/or preserved to some extent.

5. Your Legacy Is Lost

If your digital footprint is hidden behind avatars and passwords, there is a risk that your legacy will be lost. If your digital steward doesn't know your character's name on World of Warcraft or can't access your password-protected blog, it may be impossible for the person to identify and, in turn, steward, your legacy.

More importantly, the significance of your digital files may be misunderstood. Without context as to their creation and importance (or unimportance), it will be impossible for your digital steward to know what to preserve and what to delete. In the absence of guidance, your data may never be found and, if it's discovered by accident, it may still be lost in (digital) space without the connecting information that gives it meaning.

6. Neglected or Ignored: Digital Litter

As creepy as the idea of becoming a digital zombie might be, the idea of becoming digital detritus is equally unappealing. Without knowledge of the extent of your digital footprint, endless digital aspects of your life may be left untouched for eternity somewhere in cyberspace.

Digital litter will be found in your smartphone, your tablet, and your computer. It will also surface, like that horrible island of plastic refuse in the Pacific Ocean, everywhere you've worked or played online. Old documents, unfinished documents, out of focus photographs, scraps of travel itineraries and more will surface alongside more meaningful personal history, digital mementos, cultural contributions, and meaningful work.

One of the antidotes to digital litter is to organize your digital life while you're still living. Angela's book, *Declutter Your Data* (Self-Counsel Press, 2018), offers strategies to tame your virtual paper tiger. In the process, you'll do some of the work necessary to create a clear and effective digital legacy plan.

5
Digital Estate Planning

Digital estate planning requires you to go beyond your last will and testament. As discussed in Chapter 3: Assets and Access, the legal profession, estate planning associations, and levels of government worldwide are still catching up to technological advances and coming to grips with how to deal with the distribution and ownership of digital assets. In the meantime, you need to come up with an independent plan for these assets in much the same way as you would come up with a plan for your traditional estate.

You need not do this alone. This book, along with the resources we have included will provide a roadmap for you to follow as you plan. You can enlist the aid of a variety of professionals as well as consult with your legal executor or trusted friends and family members. Depending on your jurisdiction, you may be able to legally appoint a digital trustee or steward.

This plan is intended to ensure your wishes can be carried out, and that access to your online assets, private and public, is granted to the appropriate steward(s).

1. Beyond Your Last Will and Testament

In recent years, there has been a rise in something called an ethical will. According to Barry K. Baines, the author of *Ethical Wills: Putting Your Values on Paper* (Da Capo Press, 2006), "Unlike a 'last will and testament' disposing of one's estate or an advanced directive for healthcare decisions, an ethical will is not legally binding. Rather, a good ethical will transmits values, life lessons, family history, and other experiences to those left behind when the author dies. One pictures a written version of those few choice words of wisdom spoken by a family elder on his/her deathbed. While the legal will deals with material goods, the ethical will is meant to pass on the non-material goods and family traditions of equal or greater importance" (deadsocial.org)

In many ways your digital estate plan can follow along the lines of the ethical will. An ethical will is not legally binding, and nor is your digital legacy plan, but it helps to pass on a sense of what is important to you. Today, people spend so much of their lives online. If time spent is the measure of value and importance, it is fair to say that people give a high ranking to digital engagement. The investment of time goes beyond our technical digital footprints. Imparting that value to our loved ones can be partly addressed using the ethical will model. The ethical will and/or digital estate plan will act in conjunction with, not in place of your legal will.

2. Empowering Your Executor and Digital Steward

One of the best ways you can empower your executor to deal with digital matters on your behalf is to talk with the person before you die. Hopefully, the executor is already aware that you have appointed him or her to deal with your tangible assets and distribute them based on the wishes you have outlined in your legal will. The person is prepared to do this work for you in the event of your death. Your legal executor, however, may not be digitally savvy and may not be able to deal practically and technically with what is required to execute your digital legacy plan.

The job of an executor is already a difficult one, requiring extreme attention to detail, and the navigation and negotiation of family dynamics. At the same time, the person may be dealing with his or her own issues of loss and grief.

Discussing what you prefer to do with your digital assets in advance will make the person's job easier. If it makes sense, and they are different people, introduce your executor to the person you have asked to be your digital steward. The role of the digital steward is not to replace the executor, but rather to work with him or her in a complementary capacity. Get together while you are crafting your plan and create an opportunity to air concerns, or ask questions for clarification.

Your executor may well have the skills needed to successfully implement your digital legacy plan. If so, that is excellent. To empower the person, all you need to do is to make this clear in your written wishes. It is not uncommon for wills to be contested. As we noted in Chapter 3, legal mechanisms are still evolving in regard to digital ownership. Leaving clear instructions with friends, family, or your legal representative cannot guarantee your wishes will be carried out. In fact, your executor, as legal representative could potentially block your steward, but having them work together from the start, will definitely increase the odds that your digital legacy plan will be executed.

Use the Important Contacts Worksheet as shown in Sample 4 (available on the download kit) to record the names and contact information of your executor and steward, as well as others who may be useful in processing your wishes.

3. Working with Professionals

In life, you'll work with a variety of professionals to prepare and make your wishes known. In death, your executor or appointed administrator/next of kin, will work with the same professionals to carry out your wishes.

In most jurisdictions, notaries and lawyers are both empowered to create and execute the last will and testament. They may also offer complementary services to work with you to prepare a digital legacy plan or deal with digital assets. Check with your service providers to see if they have added digital estate planning to their roster. Even if they haven't, they may still be willing to work with you to expedite your wishes.

Sample 4
Important Contacts Worksheet

Important Contacts Worksheet		
	Date: April 16, 2019	
	As you prepare your digital legacy plan, it's essential to note all the important contacts that your executor or digital steward will/may need to contact.	
	Legal	
	Lawyer:	Fred Taylor 555-555-5555
	Notary:	Sylvia Armstrong
	Executor:	Sean McLeod
	Technical	
	Digital steward:	Rebecca Luxemburg
	Web master:	Nathan Coleman
	IT support:	Paul Perley
	Family & Friends	
	Spouse:	Ian
	Children:	Dom, Christina, Michael
	Trusted friend:	Darlene
	Spiritual	
	Priest/Rabbi/Imam:	Pastor Brian
	Counselor:	Jen Matt
	Personal coach:	Faye Crocker

Another expert you'll work with is a funeral director. Some people may choose to prearrange and prepay for their funeral, cremation, or burial. If not, your executor or loved ones will work with these experts to make these arrangements. Trends in memorialization and funerary services are changing, as we discuss in Chapters 7 and 8. Depending on the scope of your digital engagement in life, you may want your digital steward to work with these professionals to ensure access to digital memorabilia such as photos, videos, audio recordings or other media, as well to manage online tributes or memorial social media feeds related to your service. You will want to make this expectation clear to your steward and your executor.

If you are in a care home, hospital, or hospice, as you approach your death, your executor or steward may need to engage with the staff of these institutions. For example, perhaps you would like an end-of-life audio or video message produced while you are being cared for. You may wish to post regularly on your social media feeds while you are dying and require assistance to do so. It may be the last opportunity for you to pass on access codes, passwords, or final preferences. Your steward may need to act as an advocate on your behalf, and negotiate with your care team. Many institutions restrict the use of cell phones, or have limited Wi-Fi access. Staff or older family members may see personal technology as an unwanted intrusion at a tender time. Let your care team, your executor and/or steward, and your family know your wishes.

A new profession has appeared in recent years: The death doula, a professional to help with the practical and spiritual elements of dying. We'll share more about death doulas in Chapter 7.

No matter which expert is assisting you, it is extremely helpful if there is understanding of the deceased's wishes. A digital estate plan can be a vital document in this process.

4. There Are No Secrets in Cyberspace

Finally, making your digital estate plan is an opportunity to clean your digital closets. What's in your files that you wish you could forget? What do you want erased upon your death? Better still, what's online that you could erase now and save those left behind the discomfort of dealing with, including your digital steward or executor?

Being human, most of us will have some potentially embarrassing details about our lives or our online interactions tucked away in obscure corners of cyberspace. Think about the skeletons in your closet. Consider smartphones, computers, and tablets. You may wish to sweep and clear your browser history on these devices periodically, or leave instructions to have this done on your death. Don't forget about embarrassing apps on phones or tablets. Sweep and clear your hard drive or other storage devices such as external hard drives, thumb or flash drives, CDs or DVDs. Potentially embarrassing photos, videos, documents, or bootleg software should all be deleted on your death as well as any secret or potentially hurtful texts, iPhone or email messages, or secret accounts you may hold.

The secrets need not be illicit, illegal, or dangerous to be worth a pre-mortem purge.

A good friend of Vicki's is dealing with a challenging set of circumstances with his adult son. He frequently sends direct messages seeking advice, support, or simply to vent his frustration. These conversations are private and intended to be supportive, but should the son read them out of context, particularly while grieving, they could be hurtful. It is easy to forget that what you assume are private conversations — via text, direct message, Messenger, WhatsApp, or other platforms — are actually a part of your digital footprint and could easily be accessible after your death.

Use the Clean Your Digital Closet Worksheet to note files that you want deleted immediately upon your death and to note anything that should be shared with a limited audience.

Sample 5
Clean Your Digital Closet Worksheet

Clean Your Digital Closet Worksheet

Date: March 16, 2019

Use this page to note specific instructions for your executor or digital steward. This should include where to find originals and scans of essential documents such as birth certificates plus any special wishes you may have. This may include instructions to delete and permanently erase unfinished work, sexually explicit content, or potentially embarrassing or illegal files. Don't forget texts and private messaging services in addition to your hard drive files and email folders.

- Original documents: in safety deposit box

- Please delete file marked "Personal" in My Documents on desktop computer

- Delete WhatsApp chats with Faye Crocker and Jen Matt

6
Transitioning Social Media, Websites, and Other Tools

According to Everplans.com, an online planning and digital archiving service, there are more than 200 online platforms where user accounts are commonly set up — everything from Airbnb to Zynga. Upon your death, every online account you hold will need to be dealt with in some way by your estate, either via a plan, or through attrition.

While some of the platforms that will need the attention of your estate are obvious, such as computer and smartphone access codes, social media account passwords, and online bank accounts, nearly everyone has other common user accounts that may be less obvious. A sampling includes Amazon, Ancestry.com, Booking.com, Dropbox, iTunes, iCloud, Netflix, eBay, Etsy, Eventbrite, Evernote, Google Play … the list goes on. Depending on your professional requirements or your personal interests, the list can easily grow well into the double, or even triple, digits.

Our best advice is this: Make a list and keep it up to date. If you read and implemented the ideas in Chapter 3, you can use your Digital Assets Inventory as a good starting point for your list.

In this section we will deal with the current options for the most common social media platforms: Facebook, Twitter, Instagram, LinkedIn, Pinterest, and Snapchat as well as key web-based service providers such as Google.

Platforms and their technical features are in a continual state of evolution so we will also point you toward key guidelines that can be applied, even if the available features change (which they will, quite possibly in the time it takes you to read this chapter). Determining who can access your accounts and how that access is set up is crucial to a complete digital legacy plan. We'll discuss password managers and how they can give you and your family peace of mind now and in the event of your death.

Rights regarding legal access to digital assets vary in different countries, and often within the states and provinces within those countries. Lawmakers are working hard to define legal obligations and expectations for the online world, but much of this work is still in formative stages. Technology advances much more quickly than regulatory bodies can keep up, which is why it is so important to clearly state your wishes, either as part of your estate (please consult with an estate planner, lawyer, or notary) or entrust them to a friend or family member.

It will greatly simplify things if you use the access tools available within the platforms and ensure someone you trust has access to your login and password information.

Privacy advocates, rightly so, are pushing back in the courts as lawmakers struggle to catch up. For now, most digital platforms will not provide access information to anyone other than the direct account holder. Far better to empower yourself and those who will be tasked with taking care of these matters by setting up the necessary access and instructions in advance.

This would be a great time to get out your Digital Assets Inventory Worksheet from Chapter 3 and go through it to check and see if you have covered all your bases. Use the worksheet shown here in Sample 6 in conjunction with the Digital Assets Inventory.

1. Managing Social Media Accounts

It is good social media practice to ensure that there is always more than one administrator on an account. Regardless of whether or

Sample 6
Social Media and Other Accounts Worksheet

Social Media and Other Accounts Worksheet

Date: June 16, 2019

By this stage of your digital legacy planning, you're gathering specific details to help your executor or digital steward.

Fill out this sheet in detail and revise as you open or close accounts. Don't forget to include answers to security questions that safeguard your accounts.

Account	Desktop computer
Login	myname
Password	pw123
Wishes	access data

Account	www.mybusiness.com
Login	admin123
Password	pw456
Wishes	delete as desired

Account	domain host
Login	my name
Password	pw789
Wishes	release domain

Account	Facebook
Login	email address
Password	pw1011
Wishes	close account

Account	LinkedIn
Login	email address
Password	pw1213
Wishes	close account

Account		
Login		
Password		
Wishes		
Note any legacy contacts or administrators you may have assigned to accounts.	My daughter, Christina shares website access.	

Fill in a hard copy of this worksheet or feel free to recreate this template in your own digital document.

not you do this as part of your digital legacy planning, or as you are setting up new accounts, it simply makes sense. Glitches can occur and it is not uncommon for people to be accidentally locked out of an account. Sometimes this is the result of a technical problem, or sometimes accounts are hacked or tampered with. Having a trusted friend, colleague, or family member as a coadministrator of your accounts ensures that you can have access when you need it. This is especially important if you are using social media for business. Taking this step now will not only help safeguard your accounts, but will make the potential transition or closing of your accounts much simpler after you die.

If you are currently the caregiver of a terminally ill friend or family member, or you offer technical help and support to someone who is ailing or aging, encourage the person to take the step of adding an administrator or giving account access to an additional person now.

Most platforms are rigorous in their refusal to provide login information, which again emphasizes the value of providing your account email, password, and other login information to a trusted person before your death.

There are also documents worth mentioning that may be required at different points in the process. If you are crafting your own digital legacy plan, start putting these documents together on behalf of your estate now. You will want to include your notarized or legally registered will, with your preferences regarding your digital assets listed in writing and stored in the same location. Keep your birth certificate and marriage certificate (if applicable) stored with these documents. As an extra step, scan these documents and store them online as a password protected PDF document.

If you are managing accounts on behalf of an estate, in most cases you will need the following:

- Your full name
- The full name and email address on this person's account
- A link to the account you are dealing with
- Documentation of the death (e.g., death certificate, obituary, news article)
- Your relationship to the person with supporting documentation such as:
  - Birth or marriage certificate
  - Public mention of relationship
  - Family tree
  - Family/household records
  - Notarized proof of relationship

Typically you will not be required to provide either your own, or the deceased's Social Security (USA), or Social Insurance (Canada) Number. You may also wish to redact identifying information that is not required from the documents you submit.

Let's discuss how to deal with common social media platforms.

1.1 Facebook

At the time of this writing Facebook offers users essentially two options in the event of the death of an account holder. You (or your executor or steward) can choose to have your account permanently deleted, or you can appoint a legacy contact to look after your memorialized account. Facebook, if it becomes aware of your passing, will permanently delete your account if it has not been memorialized. You can find these options under the settings tab of your Facebook account.

A legacy contact, chosen by the account holder, ensures that your account can be managed once it's memorialized. It is not possible to add a legacy contact to an account that has already been memorialized.

The difference between a memorialized account and your current profile are significant. The word "Remembering" will appear next to your name, and the content you shared while living, such as photos and posts, remains visible to the audience it was shared with. The memorialized profile will not appear in ads or birthday reminders. Unless there is an appointed legacy contact, memorial profiles can't be changed. Memorialized accounts are subject to the privacy settings of the profile at the time the account is memorialized.

At the current time, your legacy contact can do the following:

- Write a pinned post for your profile such as a final message or obituary. As noted previously, if your timeline and tagging settings don't allow anyone other than you to post on your timeline, your legacy contact won't be able to do this either.

- Respond to new friend requests, likely to come from friends and family who may not have already been on Facebook, but who want to join in remembrance.

- Update your profile picture and cover photo.

- Request the removal of your account.

One important feature is that your legacy contact can download a copy of what you've shared on Facebook. If the intent is to eventually delete the account entirely, or remove the memorial page, the ability to download and save this content is a valuable feature, especially if you want to save these memories.

While the legacy contact has the kind of account management access listed above, there are several things the legacy contact can't do. The person will not be able to log into your account, nor can he or she remove or change past posts, photos, and other things shared on your timeline. In part this is why it is important to be judicious about what you post while you are still living. (See Chapter 7, Curating the Museum of Me).

The legacy contact also can't read your messages, remove any of your friends, or make new friend requests, or add a new legacy contact to your account. Should you require access to this kind of personal information, there is a process involving specific and valid documents such as death certificates and wills.

While friends and family can visit a memorialized account to share memories and grieve after a person has passed away, you may find creating a Facebook Group to be a more comforting and effective choice. Groups can be public, private, or secret. You may wish to memorialize your loved one's profile and create a private Facebook Group where those with close ties can connect. In Chapter 8, we offer you more insight into how to use Groups to provide comfort to you and your loved ones.

Whatever choice you make, it is important to remember that online accounts ultimately belong to the platform itself. Technology changes rapidly, and platforms such as Facebook frequently change the rules.

Essentially, there are three choices for Facebook and other similar platforms.

Assuming you have a password, you can simply sustain the personal profile. The account will continue as though the account holder is still living, which can be disconcerting and cause distress to the bereaved.

The account can be memorialized, as described above, or you can delete the account entirely, hopefully after having harvested important memorabilia.

To learn the specifics of how to select a legacy contact or request the memorialization or removal of a Facebook account, visit Facebook Help at www.facebook.com/help.

1.2 Instagram

Similarly to Facebook, Instagram accounts can also be memorialized or removed entirely. If you choose to remove an account, there is a simple online form to be completed by an immediate family member or executor. Proof of relationship and proof of death is required. Unlike Facebook, Instagram does not (at time of writing) offer a legacy contact option.

A memorialized account on Instagram remains exactly as it was, although hidden from public spaces such as Explore (a feature in Instagram that recommends accounts to follow).

The key features of a memorialized Instagram account include:

- No one can log into a memorialized account.

- The profile of a memorialized account looks the same as an account that hasn't been memorialized.

- Memorialized accounts can't be changed, including changes to likes, followers, tags, posts, and comments.

- Posts including photos and videos stay on Instagram and are visible to the audience they were shared with.

In all cases, ensuring login information for all your accounts is available to a trusted person will make undertaking these processes far easier.

> Steve Dotto has an excellent reputation for his online courses. He, too, has explored digital legacy and his free course "Your Online Legacy: Social Media After You Die" includes video screen captures showing how the legacy planning options work in many of the social media accounts we discuss in Chapter 5. It will give you a good basic reference. (dottotechu. thinkific.com/courses/your-online-legacy-social-media-after-you-die)

1.3 Twitter

At this time, Twitter has essentially only one way of handling a deceased user's account. A friend, family member, or executor makes a request supported by the appropriate documentation and Twitter will deactivate the account.

The other option is to simply leave the account as it was. However, a key concern about sustaining accounts as though the account holder is still living, is that these accounts are vulnerable to hackers, sexbots, and trolls if they are left unattended and inactive. This can be very disturbing for family, friends, fans, and followers.

To find out how to deactivate a Twitter account: https://help. twitter.com/en/managing-your-account/how-to-deactivate-twitter-account.

1.4 LinkedIn

LinkedIn does not offer a memorialization or legacy account option. LinkedIn has a request form for deactivation that requires supporting documentation. See www.linkedin.com/help/linkedin/ answer/2842/deceased-linkedin-member-removing-profile. To complete the form, you'll need the following information:

- The deceased's name as it appears on their profile

- The URL to the LinkedIn profile

- The deceased's email address

- Date of death

- Link to obituary

- Company where the deceased was most recently employed

Once the death has been verified to LinkedIn's satisfaction, the profile will be deleted.

1.5 Pinterest

Pinterest does not offer a memorialization or legacy account option. Pinterest requires you to email care@pinterest.com with your request with proof of death and your relationship to the account holder. You'll have to provide the death certificate, obituary, or a news article plus relationship proof such as marriage certificate, birth certificate, or notarized documentation of the relationship. See help.pinterest.com/en/articles/deactivate-or-close-your-account for the current acceptable documentation.

1.6 Snapchat

Perhaps it due to the general age of the Snapchat demographic, but Snapchat currently offers no special options or policies for handling a user's death. The only way to deactivate a deceased user's account is to log in and close the account.

2. Google and Other Websites

Google may have started as a simple search engine tool, but it has grown to encompass more and more of our daily digital interaction. From the storage and sharing features of Google Drive to the ubiquitous use of Gmail as a preferred email service, Google reaches deeply into the heart of our online business and personal interactions.

Google offers a tool called the Inactive Account Manager. Inactive Account Manager is a way for users to share parts of their account data or notify someone if they've been inactive for a certain period of time. As the holder of the Google account, whether for yourself or a business, you need to go to the Inactive Account Manager page (Google it — seriously!) and follow the step-by-step instructions to set up a trusted contact who will be notified if your account is inactive after the amount of time you specify. You can determine whether or not you want your trusted contact to be able to download your data — data you can identify and list. If your Google account is associated with a business, it is likely you will want the data to be available after your demise. If your account is strictly personal, this may not matter.

It is highly recommended that you set this up as part of your digital legacy plan. It may be that you are acting as the executor or steward for the deceased's digital assets. If you Google, "I am an executor and I need to access a Google account," the first statement made by Google is: "People expect Google to keep their information safe, even in the event of their death." This gives you a good indication of the kind of journey you are embarking on in dealing with digital account access, and should reinforce our message about the importance of dealing with your digital life before death.

In the event that an Inactive Account Manager has not been set up, Google will work with immediate family members and/or representatives to close the relevant accounts, and in some circumstances to provide content or data from the account. Google, and most other platforms will require proof of your identity and relationship to the account holder, as well as a copy of a death certificate in order to begin the process. Go online and check the specific requirements as they may change. Most inquiries can be initiated online and do be sure to check the specific requirements for Google or any platform you are trying to access. Prepare to be patient with the process.

You can make requests regarding setting up an Inactive Account Manager, closing an account, requesting funds, or obtaining data here: support.google.com/accounts/troubleshooter/6357590?hl=en.

> Throughout this book, we've provided links to help you find your way to the information, forms, and experts that can help you develop your digital legacy plan. Of course, we aren't in control of the entire web so the site owners may move or update their content. As a result, the links are subject to change. To find the same, updated resource, you could try a keyword search. We also invite you to join our Facebook group, Death in the Digital Age. We'll be there regularly sharing updated resources and answering community members' questions.

2.1 A Note about YouTube

YouTube, a video-sharing website, is a Google product. Typically an account can be deleted simply by logging in (you will need a username and password) and choosing the "delete channel" option.

Popular YouTube channels generate revenue through Google's AdSense program. If you, or your loved one is receiving revenue as a result of YouTube videos, you may prefer to sustain the account. Currently, if the AdSense system doesn't know that an account owner is deceased, the system will continue to make automatic payments using the payment settings in the AdSense account. If you are the rightful heir or executor and need payment of earnings to be redirected, you can make a request to Google. You will need appropriate documentation.

Please check Google Adsense current policies and procedures here: support.google.com/adsense/.

3. Password Managers

A quick glance at your Digital Assets Inventory from Chapter 3 will give you a sense of the sheer number of passwords required to engage in your daily online life. At one time, most of us had only a handful of passwords to keep track of. Now, it is possible to have hundreds. Added to passwords are usernames, multiple email addresses, and the answers to specific questions that all act as protection for online accounts and services. Plus the linked phone number(s) or other data to receive two-factor authentication codes via text message or other ways. So, how do people keep track of this plethora of information?

Some people stick with an analog approach; pencil on paper. A professional woman we know keeps a file folder in her desk drawer. It's labeled "Passwords" and inside it are bits of paper of all shapes and sizes, noting accounts, passwords, and usernames. It's not the most elegant solution, but in the event of her death, it will make her executor's job easier. Many people write passwords on post-it notes, record them on spreadsheets, or stuff them into journals or diaries.

This kind of record-keeping is adequate if you are the only one who needs to access this information and you know exactly where to find that particular sticky note or file folder. It's woefully inadequate for your executor, or a grieving friend or family member, who may need access. As well, paper records are vulnerable to fires, floods, and traditional thievery.

A digital solution is more easily shared and back-up copies can be saved in multiple locations. Vicki and her husband keep a record of accounts using a Word document matrix stored in a shared Dropbox as a master list. A spreadsheet would work as well, if you prefer. Dropbox is a secure cloud storage, syncing, sharing, and backup service. In the matrix, accounts are listed alphabetically and passwords, usernames, email addresses, and key questions and answers are recorded as needed for each entry. At last count there were 140 entries covering both business and personal accounts. Each time an account is added or changed, the master list is updated. The advantage to this system is that the information is accessible to them at all times, from all devices and from remote locations. The disadvantage is that, despite the security offered by the cloud service provider (in this case, Dropbox), their information could be vulnerable to a coordinated hack. This system is also largely manual.

In working through her own digital legacy plan, Vicki and her husband added an extra column to their password matrix entitled "Instructions on death/incapacity." In that column they note whether the accounts are personal or professional and legacy preferences for each. A hard copy of the master list is stored in a fireproof lockbox along with master computer passwords, their legal will, a list of personal bequests, passports, birth certificates, business incorporation documents, and marriage certificates. Copies of these documents are also filed online. They have also kindly included the names and contact information of their lawyer, notary, and technical support person. In a sense, they have created an "in case of death kit" for easy access.

The information you gather for your digital legacy plan can also be a useful reference in your emergency kit. If you should have to evacuate on short notice, these details can help you connect to your digital life from any computer. That's a helpful thing, especially if your computer stayed behind in the path of the forest fire, hurricane, or flood.

As an option, password managers, or password wallets, are a digital solution to help you securely keep track of sensitive information. Typically, they only require you to remember one master password to access all your accounts. The master password acts as a kind of "key to the castle." Utilizing simple browser plugins or downloadable smartphone apps, password managers save your usernames and passwords as you log into various websites. A password generator creates complex, unique passwords as you create accounts. In theory, these passwords are more secure because of their length and complexity. As block chain becomes more widely used, password managers will likely be further secured with this new type of encryption.

There are a number of service provides in the password management game. These are four of the more popular ones:

- 1Password (1password.com)

- Dashlane (www.dashlane.com)

- KeePassX (www.keepassx.org)

- LastPass (www.lastpass.com)

Prices for the services vary. 1Password charges a monthly fee of $2.99 USD for a single user and $4.99 USD for a family of five. Dashlane offers a free service for up to 50 stored passwords and a paid package at $3.33 USD/month. KeePassX is open source software available for free but it requires some technical know-how. LastPass offers a free basic account. Premium services are also available for a fee of $2/month for one user and $4/month for up to six users in a family. Small businesses and enterprise level packages are also available from 1Password and LastPass. **Note:** These prices were current as of October 2018.

While a digital system has many advantages, there can be flaws in the digital system, too. You may be concerned about putting "too many eggs in one basket," as the old adage goes. If you're new to digital you might goof as you set up your password account creating access problems later on. It can also be hard to incorporate additional useful information into a password manager. Just as we've recommended for your digital assets list, it can be useful to note which accounts are important and which are not. You may also want to note the answers to challenge questions, two-factor authentication codes, or other related details.

It's also important to reflect on current encryption standards. They may be sufficient for now but will be insufficient in future to secure your information. Relying on digital system requires you to trust that the system will continue to exist. If the company fails, will your data be purchased by a competitor worthy of your trust or farmed out in a digital garage sale to the highest bidder?

Of course, there's tremendous advantage to the convenience of having to remember just one master password. You're not likely to spill coffee on that mental piece of paper as you would if your password notes are tucked under your keyboard (a common practice amongst those who prefer analog). It's much easier to keep a single current password updated in any digital legacy documentation you're preparing and maintaining for your digital steward.

No system is perfect, nor is any system completely secure. Much like if you were to have your wallet or credit cards stolen, your first step is to contact the service providers and have your cards canceled. In the event of an online hack of your digital assets, or should paper copies of passwords and records be stolen, your first step is to go onto your most sensitive and high-risk accounts (online banking, tax accounts, etc.) and immediately change your passwords. As well, you will want to notify service providers of the breach.

Nevertheless, what is important is that you have a system and that someone knows how to access it.

4. Access to the Management of Other Websites

If you own one or more websites, you will want be sure that username and login information is available in your master password list to your executor or steward. As well, make a note of the domain host, domain registrar, and any associated email addresses or passwords for the hosting account. Remember that your domain host and domain registrar might be two separate companies, although many offer both services.

If you have left instructions for your executor or steward to follow, the person will know whether or not you want your website to remain active after death, to be taken down from the internet, and/or to have some form of notice or obituary on your site.

Much will depend on the role that digital played in your life while you were living. As we noted earlier, if you are an online influencer, advocate for social causes, or produce creative work or digital content, you will likely want your contributions and the websites that support that work to continue to be a source of information, service and support beyond your death. If your website supports or promotes a business, it is a digital asset that will be part of a professional legacy or succession plan. You may choose to only have parts of your website remain active after you are gone, or you may wish to transition your website off the internet after a certain period of time.

Please be sure to leave a clear set of instructions for your digital steward to follow to access the dashboard of your website in order to delete or revise posts as per your wishes. If you are taking care of website(s) on behalf of a friend or loved one, you will need to have the username and password to access the site itself in order to make changes.

To delete the site, or to sell or sustain the URL (Uniform Resource Locator, or the unique website address) you will need to contact the domain host and the domain registrar, if separate. Most domain contracts are prepaid annually and come up for automatic renewal based on the term for which the URL has been purchased. If you cancel credit cards or close the deceased's PayPal account, you may inadvertently put the domain at risk.

It is not uncommon for people, especially active content creators and rising influencers, to own one or more domains that are not yet in use. As you write your plan, or investigate domain ownership on behalf of an estate, you will want to search also for these unused URLs.

There are a number of common website building and blogging platforms. It will help your digital steward if you note whether your website is hosted or self-hosted. Hosted websites are built through services like WordPress.com, Blogger.com, Weebly.com, SquareSpace.com, and others. A hosted website may use a hosted URL such as yourwebsite.wordpress.com or a custom URL such as yourwebsite.com. Hosted websites are popular because they are quick and easy to set up. They offer many templates and WYSIWYG (what you see is what you get) design options so that novice website creators can give their content a custom look and feel. The basic service is often free and added features are available for a modest fee.

Self-hosted websites offer more control. The website owner has access to all of his or her website files and the server(s) where data is stored. Self-hosted sites offer more opportunities for customization and typically default templates are modified to reflect the brand of the individual, project, or company. Commonly used hosting companies include GoDaddy, BlueHost, HostGator, EasyDNS, and dozens of others.

There is frequent confusion about the distinctions between hosted and self-hosted websites built on the WordPress platform. Hosted sites can be found through WordPress.com while self-hosted sites use the crowdsourced software available at WordPress.org. The latter is not a hosting service but rather a portal for self-hosted WordPress site creators (or their web designers) to access and collaborate on this community built software and all its related plug-ins.

The experts at both hosted and self-hosted website companies will work with your executor or digital steward upon your death. Most require proof of death (i.e., a copy of the death certificate) and proof of identity (the executor's government issued identification such as a driver's license or passport). In addition, they may ask for further details such as the email address used by the deceased.

Some services have explicit information on their websites about what to do in case of death. Others have not published this detail but staff are available through regular customer support channels to assist you through email, webform, and/or online chat. To help you get started, here are some useful links for commonly used website services:

Hosted

- WordPress.com
  https://en.support.wordpress.com/deceased-user/

- Blogger.com
  https://support.google.com/accounts/troubleshooter/
    6357590?hl=en

- Weebly.com
  https://hc.weebly.com/hc/en-us/articles/216894527-
  How-Do-I-Delete-My-Weebly-Account-

- SquareSpace.com
  https://support.squarespace.com

Self-hosted

- GoDaddy
  ca.godaddy.com/help/how-to-gain-access-to-do
  mainsaccounts-after-owners-death-8356

- BlueHost
  my.bluehost.com/cgi/help/122#hosting

- Hostgator
  support.hostgator.com

- EasyDNS
  fusion.easydns.com/Knowledgebase/List

All of these services will work with you as you execute the wishes of your loved one. Some will respond compassionately. Others may have staff who have not been trained in how to deal with a death. As always, be prepared to be patient.

5. Other Online Accounts

In Chapter 3: Assets and Access, we offered a comprehensive list of digital assets such as servers, websites, email accounts and databases, productivity services, and gaming and entertainment accounts. Hopefully, you used the worksheet available on the download kit and created a Digital Assets Inventory while going through that chapter. You can use that now to deal with other online accounts.

Here are a few key points to consider:

- Should this account remain online?

- Is it part of my/my loved one's personal or professional legacy?

- Are there earnings or intellectual properties associated with this account?

- How should the estate deal with these earnings or potential earnings from future publication/distribution?

- Have I checked the policies and procedures related to this account?

Once you have created and gone through the Digital Assets Inventory, and the questions above, read through the Basic Guidelines in section 6. to help you navigate the process.

6. Basic Guidelines for Transitioning Accounts

If you are preparing your own digital legacy plan, decide in advance how you want each of your social media or other accounts handled: preserved as they are, deleted, memorialized, or harvested and then deleted. Make these wishes known in your digital will or to a trusted friend or family member. Compile all your login information for each account and ensure it is left in a secure location or with a trusted person.

If you are acting on behalf of an estate, or for a friend or loved one, use our checklist to ensure that you have the correct documentation, and a complete list of the digital assets that you will be responsible for taking care of.

Remember that the simplest way to deal with these accounts is if you have direct login information. Most platforms offer an online process to request the management or deletion of deceased accounts. Have your documentation ready, and be in the right frame of mind to take on this task when you sit down to do it. Patience will be required.

If you are downloading or harvesting photos, posts, links, or other memorabilia from the sites of your loved one, decide in advance how you want to file and store this information. Who is it being circulated to? How is it going to be used? This will help you as you sit down to deal with the accounts.

Angela's book *Declutter Your Data* (Self Counsel Press, 2018) is an excellent resource jam-packed with tips on dealing with the sorting, harvesting, and storing of data. You can find it here: angelacrocker.com/declutteryourdata/

Most important is that you understand the wishes of your loved one. If you know that at some point you are going to be dealing with the accounts of someone in your life — a good friend, spouse, parents, siblings, workmates, or others — start considering the personal and practical elements of their digital social media life before death. Start the conversation now, so you will be prepared later.

7
Online Memorial Planning

As digital memorials become increasingly common, it's helpful to look at the memorial from two perspectives: author and audience. Wendy Moncur and David Kirk explored this distinction in their presentation "An Emergent Framework for Digital Memorials" (DIS 2014, Jun 21-25, 2014, Vancouver, BC, Canada). The author is the creator of the memorial while the audience is the consumer.

The author might be the deceased person who has prepared a missive for posthumous publication (something that you could include in your digital legacy plan). If that is not the case, then a family member, friend, or colleague will author the memorial. The author may publish it independently or, more commonly, publish it in consultation with the executor or steward. While we're talking about an author, the memorial does not have to be text. It might be a display of personal effects, a photograph collection, a video montage, or other media.

The memorial is only effective if it is consumed by an audience. Family and friends might interact with the memorial at a funeral or memorial service. The audience can be much larger if the memorial is in words, images, or video published online. By publishing it online, the memorial is much more accessible and can reach a larger audience anywhere in the world that has an internet connection.

In the digital age, our social media feeds and websites are part of the ongoing story of our lives. After our deaths they can become a place where loved ones can gather virtually to remember, grieve, and celebrate. The way we mourn is being changed and influenced by our online interaction.

1. Digital Memorials

There are many choices around creating an online presence for a loved one after the person has died. As noted in the previous chapter, some social media platforms allow for a memorialization option or feature that enables family and friends to commemorate and share stories and remembrances of their loved one. Most funeral homes offer the option to create a digitized book of condolences, and many offer memorial websites as part of their service package.

There are also independent memorial website services available. While the quality, user-friendliness, and overall attractiveness of the websites vary by provider, most offer a relatively common set of features including sections to upload and view photos, videos, memories and stories, tributes and condolences, and a guest book. Most are simple to use and easy to set up. Some offer additional features such as musical selection, candle or ribbon offerings, or special rates or designations for those who served in the military. There are also emerging online services (see Chapter 1) devoted to providing digital legacy services and offering simple building tools to craft a memorial. One such service, based in the UK, is deadsocial.org.

Some sites are free, but most charge either a monthly, annual, or one-time fee. If you are website savvy, or know someone who is, it is also possible to build your own memorial website for a loved one. At the time of this writing, specific themes and templates for legacy sites are sparse, but a good web developer can easily craft an appropriate template. Pick a theme, color scheme, and design elements that suit the deceased person. A self-hosted site is an option, particularly if you want maximum control over the content.

A distinct advantage of creating a memorial website is ease of access to friends or family from around the world. Visitors do not need to be particularly social media or digitally savvy to visit the site or to leave messages or post stories and memories. It provides a centralized online space to store memories, share stories, and find comfort. In Chapter 5, we talk about how to access website domains if you are choosing to memorialize an existing website as a legacy site.

In her article, "Dearly Departed: Communicating with the Dead in the Digital Age" (*International Journal of Anthropology*, 2017), Jennifer Huberman explores how the internet is reshaping relationships between the living and the dead. She argues that "online memorials serve both a commemorative and a 'communicative' function, allowing for relationships with the deceased to be maintained and for connections to be made with the living others." In this way we find both comfort in the company of others who share our loss and a sense of ongoing connection with those who are gone.

The notion of an ongoing connection with those who have passed on is not necessarily a new concept. In his article, "New mourners, old mourners: online memorial culture as a chapter in the history of mourning" (*New Review of Hypermedia and Multimedia*, 2015), Tony Walter of The Centre for Death and Society explores how online and offline mourning differ and offers a brief history of mourning from preindustrial times until present day.

He notes that largely in the twentieth century, "mourners talked to the dead in private, whether silently or aloud when no-one else was around (whether at home or at the graveside)." Today, the bereaved who post on social media sites or memorial websites do so with the knowledge that their posts are public. He notes Kasket (2012) as finding that on Facebook considerably more people directly address the dead as "you" than had been found on an earlier generation of memorial sites. Interestingly, he adds, the more formal the site and/or the relationship the more likely the pronouns of she or he (or presumably "they") are used. Pervasive social media use is changing how we engage with grief and the bereaved.

We will explore dealing with death in the twenty-first century in the next chapter, but for now it is worth considering what kind of digital memorial tribute you would prefer for yourself or for a loved one. Here are a few key questions to inform your decision-making:

- Are the family, friends and loved ones digitally savvy? Will they be able to participate in online remembrances? Will they want to?

- Is the online memorial the sole opportunity to express thoughts and condolences? Will some friends or family members, for example, older, non-digital parents or grandparents be excluded?

- Who will maintain the domain, and manage and/or monitor the memorial site and/or memorialized social media accounts?

The online space is public space. If you (or the person you are acting for) or the family are very private, an online memorial may be entirely inappropriate. As well, having control over the public space may be difficult. This is especially true in the case of the death of a young person, or deaths in tragic or unusual circumstances. You may find that online friends and followers of the deceased begin actively posting and expressing their grief and loss before close friends and family are ready to deal with it.

In 2015, Vicki lost a dear friend and mentor. She died in a foreign country after a relatively short illness, and communication with the family was difficult. No formal announcement was made of her death, and although Vicki was very close to the family, the first notification of her death came via a Facebook post from someone who lived nearby. Online condolences, and expressions of shock and grief soon flooded the feeds. "It was as though crowds of people, many of whom didn't really know her, or who had not been in touch for years, were suddenly clamoring in the space. There was no time to even absorb the shock of her loss. In a way her death was public before many people even knew how sick she had been. I felt robbed of the opportunity to express grief privately. It was a terrible feeling, and if it was terrible for me, I can't imagine what it must have been like for the family," says Vicki.

To this date, Vicki's friend's account has not been memorialized. Facebook friends and family post birthday wishes, and condolences on her feed on the anniversary of her death, but there has been no formal memorialization in the online space. Before her death, no plan had been put in place to deal with the digital aspects of her life after her death.

There are many who feel that expressions of grief online are superficial, and trolls or others may use memorial sites to offer opinions on and evaluate the quality of the condolences offered. This can add further distress to the already grieving friends and family members of the deceased. There are others who simply prefer to grieve or to offer respects privately. Online tributes can create social pressure to make private feelings public.

You need to be aware that the norms and etiquettes around death and dying are changing, both online and off. As individuals, and as a society, we are grappling with changing expectations and establishing new norms in the digital space. Digital legacy planning, whether for yourself or on behalf of loved ones requires sensitivity, patience, and readiness.

We found the Everplan.com website a particularly good resource. You can find it here:

www.everplans.com

For specific insight on planning memorial websites:

www.everplans.com/articles/the-top-10-online-memorial-websites

2. Social Media Obituaries

Historically, death notices or obituaries were published in newspapers. If the death involves a celebrity or other notable person, announcements may also be broadcast on radio or television. Typically, a death notice provides very basic and somewhat scant information, while an obituary offers more detailed personal information. In both cases the purpose is to notify the community about the death and impart information as to memorial or funeral arrangements and preferred tributes, for example, flowers or a donation to a cause.

Although such notices were once commonly published in newspapers large and small, in the digital age, this practice has declined in popularity. The cost to place an obituary in most markets is high, and the traditional print industry — magazines and newspapers — is itself in decline. It is far more common now to receive the news of a death via digital channels — email, Facebook, Twitter, an online news service, or via a link or announcement from a memorial site.

Past practice is that a friend or family member composed the obituary after the death of a loved one. A new trend is emerging where people are writing or recording their own obituaries or post-mortem messages, obviously before they die, and posting them or leaving them in the care of their estate. These obituaries are often sassy, funny, and inspiring.

It is also not uncommon in the online world for an especially well-written, touching, or witty obituary to "go viral." Because information posted online is largely public, obituaries or memorial tributes are reposted and shared, sometimes by millions. This is something to consider if privacy is a concern.

Whether you choose to prepare your own obituary or you have the task of writing one on behalf of a deceased friend or family member, there are a few key points to consider. For either a death notice or an obituary, do consult with family and friends as to content and tone. A death notice, by nature, is concise and factual, but an obituary is a more expanded personal account, and as a result often reflects the personality of the deceased.

For example, when Vicki's father died she wrote a funny limerick-style poem about him, describing some of his obvious personality tics. The poem was included in his printed obituary as it neatly captured recognizable aspects of his character, particularly his quirky sense of humor. For the family, humor is an important shared value and memorializing this aspect of his personality was important to them. For someone less quirky, a more formal poem, or no poem at all may be more appropriate.

Consulting with friends and family will not only ensure an accurate and meaningful obituary, it will also help those grieving to process thoughts and feelings. It offers an opportunity for their memories and perspectives to be honored and expressed.

Keep in mind that unofficial or unauthorized memorial posts may appear on one or more social media channels. These posts may be created by someone connected to the deceased with good intentions. Angela had a 35-year-old friend, Colleen, die of cancer and a well-meaning work colleague felt compelled to participate in the charitable CIBC Run for the Cure, in support of the Canadian Cancer Society, in her memory. Colleen's family was initially upset when the colleague started the fundraising campaign but later came to take comfort in the efforts of the memorial runners and the substantial donations they gathered. Other times unexpected memorial posts might be triggered by peripheral mourners or people who hear about the death through news media. Lisbeth Klastrup, a Danish researcher, conducted a study looking at public memorial pages on Facebook (" 'I didn't know her, but …' Parasocial mourning of mediated deaths on Facebook RIP pages," *New Review of Hypermedia and Multimedia*, 2015). She concluded "that public RIP pages might be understood as virtual spontaneous shrines." In a sense, this is the digital equivalent of a roadside floral tribute.

Assuming you're writing the official death notice or obituary, you may want to include the following information:

- The name (first and last) of the deceased (and nickname, if applicable).

- The year and location of birth and the date and location of death.

- Date, time, and location of the memorial or funeral service, viewing or visitation, and reception (if there is one).

- The name of a charity to which donations should be made in the deceased's name and whether donations are in lieu of flowers.

- A short summary of surviving immediate family members (e.g., spouse, children, and grandchildren).

- A short thought about the deceased; for example, "He was well loved by his family and peers" or "Her accomplishments were widely recognized in her industry."

The points above cover the details that should be in a death notice. For an obituary or a more expanded written tribute, consider adding the following:

- A general indication of the nature of death (i.e., whether it was a sudden passing or after a long illness). For example, "after a courageous battle with cancer."

- A list of survivors, starting with spouse, children, and grandchildren, followed by siblings and other immediate family members.

- A list of immediate family members that predeceased the deceased.

- Biographical details such as —

  - education;

  - career achievement;

  - military, civic, or humanitarian service;

  - hobbies, clubs, or other interests;

  - special memories or descriptions of the deceased's character or personality; and

  - a favorite poem or quotation.

These points apply whether you are preparing the obituary for an online outlet or for more traditional media, such as newspapers. The difference, aside from medium, is in the cost. You will pay per column inch in most newspapers, although costs for obituary space vary. A digital or social media obituary is typically a cost-free option, in that the only cost associated are already covered in the platform subscription or hosting fee. The digital space is essentially limitless so you are free to include as many memories or as much detail as you (and friends and family) are comfortable with. Depending on the mediums in which you choose to publish, you may want to craft a short version for print purposes and a more comprehensive version for the memorial website or social media.

One cautionary point: Be careful not to include any details that may result in identity theft. For example, omit the deceased's middle name, maiden name, exact birthdate, or home address.

Use the Writing an Obituary Worksheet (available on the download kit, shown in Sample 7) to draft the obituary of a loved one or to compose one for yourself before you die.

Another advantage of the online or social media obituary is that the notification is almost instantaneous. Website or social media posts are easily shared with a quick copy and paste of a link, or a click on a "share" button. As mentioned in the Digital Memorials section, the interactive nature of the digital space enables engagement and shared grief. Social media obituaries create a kind of techno-spiritual space where memories, anecdotes, and additional

Sample 7
Writing an Obituary Worksheet

<table>
<tr><td rowspan="6">**Writing an Obituary Worksheet**</td><td>Date: July 16, 2019</td></tr>
<tr><td>Use this worksheet to draft an obituary for a loved one or to compose one for yourself before you die. Note if you wish the death to be announced publicly on social media feeds or elsewhere online.</td></tr>
<tr><td>Please do not announce my death online, unless doing so for your own comfort.</td></tr>
<tr><td>In my obituary highlight how much I loved my family, my work, and my hobbies, I especially treasured my glass blowing group of friends and the career opportunities offered by my women mentors.</td></tr>
<tr><td>No flowers please, online donations can be made to the church.</td></tr>
<tr><td>Please use the professional headshot taken in our last family photo session. It is the one used on my LinkedIn account.</td></tr>
</table>

details about the life and death of the individual can be publicly shared and distributed.

Don't forget about notifying other online groups, clubs, or gaming communities about the death of your loved ones. As we mentioned in Chapter 3, if the deceased played World of Warcraft for years, their in-game friends will grieve for their avatar.

In a way, the digital world is giving new life to obituaries and altering the way they are written. They can be witty, entertaining, deeply personal, and sometimes even blunt. What's important is that the obituary is respectful of the deceased, meaningful to family and friends, and a true reflection of the character and life of the person it honors.

3. Curating the Museum of Me

Vicki contends in her book *#Untrending*, that we can, and should, be conscious and intentional about what we post on our social media feeds, and be mindful about the kind of online commentary we offer on news items and in chat groups. If we carefully consider the tone and perspective of the online content we produce: blogs, vlogs, videos, and stories, it will be easier for our loved ones to make choices about what will remain online after we are gone.

In her book, Vicki quotes her lifelong friend, Darlene Barnes Rosner, who had this to say about her Facebook posts: "I love that all of my posts are like an ever-growing ongoing time capsule of what I am thinking, seeing, and posting about. It is the Museum of Me and I have filled it myself. Everything I post has been my choice, what I want to show about myself."

Vicki's book *#Untrending: A Field Guide to Social Media That Matters, How to Post, Tweet & Like Your Way to a More Meaningful Life* (First Choice Books, 2016) is full of insight on ways to use social media mindfully. Find it here: www.vickimcleod.com/the-book/

Thinking about your public online engagement as the "Museum of Me" helps you curate as you go. This kind of thoughtful approach will not only improve the quality of what is shared online overall, it helps you to identify what really matters to you. In a sense, those of you who have online profiles on platforms such as Facebook, Twitter, and Instagram have become curators of your own personal museums. Approaching your online practices this way, you can choose to post what you feel is central to who you really are, what is meaningful, or significant. You also create a record of the everyday — the brands you use, the places you frequent, the small repeated experiences of daily living. In doing so, you craft newsfeeds that reflect your legacy while you are living. Using Darlene's example, she is already considering what her newsfeed says about her and her life. It will therefore, be somewhat easier for her surviving family to accept her digital legacy as is. What we don't know is what may be contained in her private messages and texts. They may cover more private or painful aspects of her life, not what she has curated for public consumption.

If you are thinking about your personal social media practices in the context of digital legacy — your "museum of me" — you are in a good position to begin thinking about going a step further. That is, self-memorialization.

While self-memorialization may sound both egotistical as well as slightly morbid, thinking about your online habits this way will help you plan and manage your online presence to be an accurate reflection of who you are. As well, you will get in the habit of weeding through what you post, save, and store online in much the same way as you might weed through your storage closets or prune down a treasured collection. As a conscientious curator you can start to determine what is worth keeping and what is extraneous.

Curation itself is the selection, management, and preservation of a collection. In this case the collection is the mass of digital content created in a lifetime. This collection becomes the source of establishing the narrative of your life.

Val Patenaude, the Director of Museum and Archives for the local historical society in Vicki's community advises the following in regard to managing personal curation, whether your own or on behalf of a deceased person. Says Patenaude, "I'm inclined to keep more rather than less, if you are not dealing with an issue of space. Keep as much as you possibly can. Remove what you think might be deeply embarrassing or illegal as it adds nothing positive to your family's universe and it can haunt you."

Patenaude does not recommend sanitizing or attempting to re-write the deceased's life (or your own, for that matter). Because we post content on the fly, it is important to put the content into some kind of context for those who will visit the newsfeed later. Attitudes and opinions make up the personality of individuals, and our online engagement tells the story of who we are (or were). If some online behavior is embarrassing or inexplicable, as the post-mortem curator you can attempt to explain it or at least provide context for it.

Start with a timeline for major life events or milestones. Those set the stage and help establish context. Then cover the individual's passions and enthusiasms. What was the person keen about, outside of his or her work? What really mattered to this person? Include professional and personal achievements, along with anecdotes from others. Try for a balance in favor of the positive. Referencing the obituary can be useful here. See Sample 8.

Everyone has a unique and interesting perspective on life, along with a distinctive point of view. Keep the quirky and honor the individuality of your loved one.

Of course, this kind of curation is most easily done for ourselves. Providing you have access, you may be acting in this capacity for someone else after he or she is gone, or possibly dealing with digital legacy in a collaborative way with a terminally ill or very elderly friend or relative. The insights offered here will help you choose what to keep and what to delete. They are also useful if you are the one creating or contributing to an online memorial of some kind.

In Angela's first book, *The Complete Idiot's Guide to Creating a Social Network* (Alpha Books, 2011), she introduced the need to think about what is public and what is private in our online profiles. She also highlighted that some information is necessary to make a person fulsome, approachable, and real. She expanded that work in *Declutter Your Data* (Self-Counsel Press, 2018), with an approach to privacy called The 3Ps. They are public, private, and personal. It's a useful framework for deciding what to share online and what to keep offline. In the context of digital legacy planning, it's a way to quickly assess what you want to share online or keep offline when a loved one dies. It can also act as a guide for curating your own newsfeeds while you are living. If you're writing a plan for your own death, you can articulate your wishes in life.

Public content includes all the details available to anyone who looks for them. It's the polished and curated information people will find online if they do an internet search. Examples include your professional work, support for charitable causes, and media reports. In grief, you may choose to reach out publicly to share your experience or to seek comfort. Practicality may also have you

Sample 8
Personal Milestones Worksheet

Personal Milestones Worksheet

Date: September 16, 2019

Use this worksheet to map your personal milestones; the narrative of your life. What are your significant milestones?

Birth	**Childhood**
1960 7 lbs. 2 oz. healthy baby	summers at the lake loved school

Coming of Age	**Marriage/Significant Other**
Prom at 16	Ian: 1982

Children	**Education/credentials**
3	BA from University of Chicago 1982

Career achievements	**Personal achievements**
Hired at XYZCorp 1984 Became GM in 1995	Marathon 1998, 2000, 2010

Retirement	**Medical**
N/A	N/A

Awards & honors	**Other**
Glassblowing award Lay service award from church	

post funeral or memorial service details publicly to inform friends and family.

In contrast, private information stays offline. You may choose to keep your tax troubles, medical conditions, and custody arrangements offline. When someone dies you may choose to keep details of the death private out of respect or so that you can grieve without an audience. Or you could share the death online to seek and, hopefully, find comfort online amongst your personal list of connections (friends, family, and colleagues).

The third "p" — personal — is where individuality can shine. Your personal content might include the hobbies or passions you pursue, or your opinions on current events. It can also highlight information that is part of your legacy but might be hard for family and friends to learn. As the #metoo movement surged to make headlines in the summer of 2018, Angela posted a never before shared example of her own first experience of unwanted sexual advances on Facebook. At the time of the incident, a boy in her Grade 9 drama class grabbed her breasts during an improv game called Murder in the Dark. Angela's story was a mild tale of assault but it had a big impact on her family. Her father, one of her Facebook friends, read about the incident 30 years after the fact. This was the first he'd heard of it and he struggled to know how to respond. The post sparked a private conversation about how a father could address such a sobering truth about his daughter's life. Angela, for her part, didn't consider the impact this addition to her digital legacy would have on her father. More generally, every post has the potential to be revealing to future generations.

Consider your own privacy preferences in the Privacy Preferences Worksheet as shown in Sample 9.

Start now to curate and streamline your own online content and craft your "museum of me." Consider whether the content is professional, private, or personal. Ask yourself if you are painting a true picture of yourself, one that can stand the test of time. Be sure that major milestones and achievements are acknowledged. Follow the same principles if you are acting on behalf of a loved one. Be sure to create a list of the most important digital memorabilia and where it can be found whether on social media feeds, in computer folders, or stored on hard drives. Reference Sample 10 (worksheets can be found on the download kit).

Sample 9
Privacy Preferences Worksheet

Privacy Preferences Worksheet

Date: August 16, 2019

Self-define elements of your life in terms of privacy. Recall the 3Ps: public, private, and personal.

Public	Work — for example, LinkedIn bio
	Glassblowing awards
	Running achievements
Private	Health — breast cancer scare 2015
	Anxiety issues — 1995
	Tax troubles — 2000
Personal	Married with children
	Hometown
	Loves glass art, outdoors, and volunteering at the church

Sample 10
Museum of Me Worksheet

Museum of Me Worksheet

Date: October 16, 2019

Use this sheet to make notes about your life. Use text, doodles, stickers, anything that you like, to represent things in your life. You can also use this worksheet to list important memorabilia and where it can be found online.

Note: Family photos on Facebook are also in the "Photos" folder of my computer

Family history records are in the "Genealogy" folder of my computer

Favorite quotes: "I'm not allowed to run with scissors. Now I play with fire and broken glass."

"Finishing a marathon is a state of mind that says anything is possible."

8
Death and Dying in the Digital Age

One of the hurdles in dealing with digital legacy planning is overcoming the taboo of death. We talked about this, at least in terms of the perspectives held by most North Americans and many western Europeans, in our opening chapter. We've found, even as authors on the subject, that we needed to overcome our own barriers and had to be willing to examine our own beliefs and preferences. Talking or writing about death and dying can trigger a whole host of emotions, and reopen past personal experiences of grief and loss.

Dealing with death in the twenty-first century presents its own set of challenges. In addition to, or possibly because of, extensive access to the internet, trends and practices in funeral and memorial services are changing. The grieving process, once a very private affair, especially for those of us born in the twentieth century, is becoming more public, returning us to a kind of collective community mourning enabled by the internet and reminiscent of pre-industrial culture.

1. Dealing with Death in the Twenty-first Century

Tony Walter, in his examination of online memorial culture in the context of the history of mourning, points us to four social contexts for mourning: family/community, private, public, and online. ("New mourners, old mourners: online memorial culture as a chapter in the history of mourning," *New Review of Hypermedia and Multimedia*, 2015.)

He compares family and community contexts for mourning in preindustrial times to the community-oriented approach emerging in modern online communities. In preindustrial times, families were large and communities were small and largely rural. Mortality rates among children were high, and the tolling of the church bell notified the community that a member had been lost. Even if the deceased or bereaved were not well known to all residents of the village or town, the community mourned together. The family and members of the community were intimately involved with caring for the corpse, and engaging in rituals and observances, religious or otherwise.

In the twentieth century, urbanization became the norm and families spread out. Healthcare improved and infant and child mortality rates dropped. Families themselves became smaller and deaths more typically occurred among the elderly, less so among younger people. The chief mourners — adult children, work colleagues, and close friends — were more fragmented geographically. Grief became a much more private affair, with death itself becoming more and more isolated from community discourse.

In the latter half of the twentieth century, at least in North America, death and dying were largely handled by institutions — care homes for the elderly; hospitals and hospices for the terminally ill, and commercial funeral homes, mortuaries, chapels, and crematoriums for the dead. The death industry became highly regulated and sterile, with the physical details handled mainly by strangers.

Concurrently, perhaps as a result of the move toward a very private grieving experience, the bereaved began to seek professional help, from counselors and therapists to mutual support groups. A couple we know who lost an infant son in the early '90s founded a local chapter of The Compassionate Friends, meeting weekly as they processed their own loss, and supporting others in similar circumstances. The Compassionate Friends, started in England in the late 1960s, is a mutual support group for families who have lost a child. This, and other groups like it, provide support and validation for mourners with shared loss. By the 1990s such groups began going digital, with membership unfettered by geography and virtual support available across time and space. This transition may very well mark the beginning of the reemergence of community mourning, afforded by the internet, social media, and the mobile technology it is supported by.

2. Grieving in the Virtual Community

In Chapter 2, we discussed the way that the global reach of accessible, real-time communication has made it substantially easier to foster community. Those who are active in the digital space, such as Angela and Vicki, refer to fans, friends, and followers collectively as an online community. Best practices in social media engagement dictate that a core principle of online interaction is this: While the environment you are communicating in is virtual, the relationships you are building are real. It is therefore more than possible for individuals to have developed strong personal networks with people they have never met offline. Such ties can be strong.

Digital connections allow us to maintain relationships long after our daily in-person interactions with a classmate or coworker have ceased. Facebook has facilitated an enduring friendship between Angela and a former colleague. Although they have not worked together in more than a decade, they still interact online. What's especially interesting about the relationship is that the other person uses a pseudonym online. After ten years of Facebook friendship with the pseudonym, Angela can no longer remember the person's real name. Yet, a warm and sincere friendship thrives between the two.

Strong personal relationships are also developed through communities of shared interest; the online mutual support groups mentioned previously, the gaming community, or enthusiastic hobby or cause-related groups. The loss of a key member of the community, whether in a private group, or simply as part of an expanded network of Facebook friends, will be keenly felt by those who have a relationship with that individual.

Very often the disparate parts of your life are represented by your online contacts and connections. They may not know each other, but they know you. When you die, memories, stories, and feelings about you will be shared online. In some cases, you may only be known by your avatar, or a pseudonym as in Angela's example. The scope of these networks goes far beyond the nuclear family, work colleagues, or close friends that characterized the more private grieving social circles in the twentieth century.

As Walter says, "This re-creates the community of mourning with some similarities to the pre-industrial village in which the whole range of both main and marginal mourners encounter one another through their online mourning behavior." Despite the fact that shared mourning is taking place in a virtual environment, the grief and sense of loss, like the relationship itself, is real.

3. The Dead among Us

Another aspect of the digital environment in regard to death and dying is that we are now becoming accustomed to having the dead among us. With the memorialization of social media profiles and pages, increased memorial websites, and the immortality promise of the internet, even in death you can continue to populate the daily lives of friends and family. This is a relatively new phenomenon in the postindustrial era, at least in the west.

Mortician Caitlin Doughty, founder of The Order of the Good Death and the author of *From Here to Eternity: Traveling the World to Find the Good Death* (WW Norton, 2017) explores how other cultures care for the dead. In her book she offers a compelling summary of powerful rituals almost entirely unknown in the west, including a ritual in Indonesia's Toraja involving regular interaction with corpses. There, in the time between death and the funeral, the body is kept in the home for periods that can last from several months to several years. They see death not as an impenetrable wall between the living and dead but as a line that can be transgressed.

Cyberspace may well be affording us the opportunity to permeate that border as well, at least in digital form. At a minimum, we are becoming much more accustomed to the public (online) sharing of loss and grief and to seeing and engaging with the departed in our newsfeeds.

Shifts in the way we deal with death, dying, and mourning are not just being felt in cyberspace. Traditional analog practices are changing too, certainly in North America. Land use constraints, environmental impacts, the high cost of traditional funerals, and other considerations have started a movement toward looking at new rituals and ways to deal with our mortal remains.

Alternatives to traditional burial or cremation are finding their way to the mainstream. Many in the twenty-first century are choosing options such as green burials, cryonics, or having ashes or remains integrated into natural settings — deep sea reefs or memorial parks. Some are even having ashes transformed into diamonds to be worn as jewelry.

The dying are moving from hospitals, often perceived as cold and antiseptic environments, to hospices where family and friends have the freedom to come and go and the staff are specially trained in end-of-life care. More and more people are requesting to die at home, surrounded by loved ones.

An emerging practice is that of the death midwife, or death doula. A death doula is someone who assists in the dying process, much like a typical midwife does for births. Death doulas perform many services including providing support before and just after death. Their role can be spiritual, psychological, or logistical, including helping to craft death plans, making arrangements for funerals and memorial services, and acting as an advocate on behalf of the dying and the bereaved.

If you are a *Star Trek* fan, as Vicki is, you are familiar with the concept of the holodeck. An emerging trend in the funeral industry is capitalizing on the use of technology to create a multisensory experience that shares the story of a lifetime with family and friends using video, picture-in-picture, music, sound effects, and even scents. Funeral webcasting delivers a live feed of the service over the internet for remote viewing. This allows anyone to be part of the service live, no matter where they are. The feed can also be downloaded to a DVD or archived as a permanent keepsake. In a sense, this is the funeral service, gone virtual.

Acceptable conduct at memorial events such as funerals is also in flux. Famously, President Obama was criticized for posing for selfies with fellow heads of state at the funeral for Nelson Mandela. While it was a somber occasion, it was also a celebration of Mr. Mandela's extraordinary life and accomplishments. Yet, a quick visit to Instagram will show more than half a million images hashtagged #funeral. Martin Gibbs and his colleagues researched this phenomena in their article "#Funeral and Instagram: death, social media, and platform vernacular" (*Information, Communication & Society*, 2015). They note, "Photo-sharing on Instagram is an informal, personal, idiosyncratic, and highly social practice that is readily appropriated as funerals shift from institutionalized and formal rituals to vernacular events, with individuals and their families increasingly engaging in forms of informal and personalized memorialization." In social groups where social media is the norm, social sharing becomes part of mourning and an appropriate expression of grief. Perhaps this is just the next step beyond the PowerPoint slide show included in many contemporary funeral services, or the newly emerging livestreamed funeral webcasts.

To once again quote Tony Walter, "The presence of mourning within social media designed for the living can create a tension between norms appropriate for everyday living and those appropriate for mourning." ("New mourners, old mourners: online memorial culture as a chapter in the history of mourning," *New Review of Hypermedia and Multimedia*, 2015.)

How do we deal with these tensions? As we said in our opening line: One hundred years from now, there will be one billion dead people on Facebook. How do we engage with the dead among us, even if it's only virtually?

Consider these thoughts as you work through the Personal Reflections on Death and Dying Worksheet, as seen in Sample 11 and available on the download kit.

4. Social Media and Mourning

In 2017, Vicki wrote an article in her newspaper column about the impacts of the disorganized and chaotic way information flows into our newsfeeds from our ever-expanding online networks. She said, "Scrolling through the Facebook newsfeed can be an emotional roller coaster ride. Life and death, tragedy and comedy all flow across our screens at a scale and scope that isn't really possible to consciously absorb, let alone respond to adequately." ("Will Simple

Sample 11
Personal Reflections on Death and Dying Worksheet

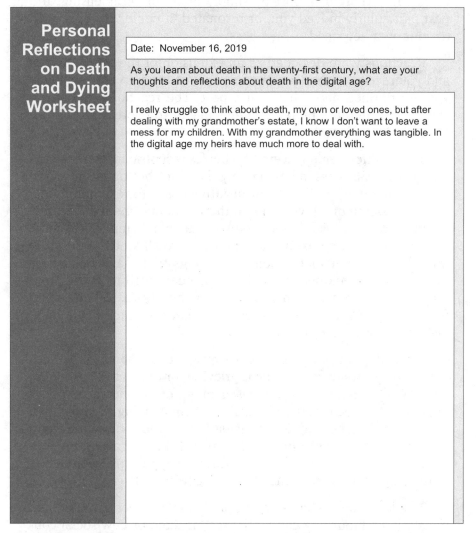

Personal Reflections on Death and Dying Worksheet

Date: November 16, 2019

As you learn about death in the twenty-first century, what are your thoughts and reflections about death in the digital age?

I really struggle to think about death, my own or loved ones, but after dealing with my grandmother's estate, I know I don't want to leave a mess for my children. With my grandmother everything was tangible. In the digital age my heirs have much more to deal with.

Emoji Reactions Reduce Our True Expressions," *Maple Ridge-Pitt Meadows News*, 2017.)

Combine the effect of the daily newsfeed roller coaster with the ever-increasing number of Facebook users who will die as time goes by, and we are faced with a true twenty-first century dilemma. How do we deal with death, dying, and grieving on social media?

Somewhere around 2016, Facebook added "reactions" to its vocabulary of responses. Prior to the reactions rollout Facebook users could reply to a post by simply liking or commenting. If a post particularly moved you, or resonated, it could also be shared to your own newsfeed.

Reactions were designed as an extension of the "like" button, and you receive a notification when they're used, in the same way you are notified about likes on a post. The reactions lexicon includes six different animated emojis meant to express Like, Love, Haha, Wow, Sad, or Angry.

The reactions emojis were Facebook's response to users reporting the awkwardness in having only the "like" button as an option when responding to difficult or negative posts, for example, posts about the death of a loved one. In their announcement of the new reactions feature, Facebook product manager Sammi Krug said, "When people come to Facebook, they share all kinds of different things, things that make them sad, things that make them happy, thought-provoking, angry. We kept hearing from people that they didn't have a way to express empathy." (https://newsroom. fb.com/news/2016/02/news-feed-fyi-what-the-reactions-launch-means-for-news-feed/)

Is clicking an emoji an adequate way to respond empathetically to the news that someone is grieving, or to react to a personal loss? With or without an increased range of emoticons, expressing more nuanced emotional reactions is challenging. Compassion, empathy, tenderness, relief, anticipation — these are subtle and sometimes complex sentiments. In times of shock, if a death is sudden, or in the freshness of grief, finding a way to express ourselves or to respond to expressions of grief is enormously challenging.

To add to the challenge, an unpredictable aspect of online and social media mourning can be the reconnected or new social connections amongst mourners. As Tony Walter notes in his article "Communication media and the dead: from the Stone Age to Facebook," "Social network sites such as Facebook can bring back into contact, after death as in life, diverse members of a person's different networks" (*Mortality*, 2015). We talked about this earlier in this chapter. Work colleagues might connect with extended family members; high school friends might connect with family elders. While everyone is united in their grief for the deceased, the social interactions in person and online can be awkward, uncomfortable, and stilted.

As it is, we often find ourselves tongue-tied at important moments. We fail to speak the words we want to say to loved ones or to the bereaved even under more traditional circumstances. We are prone to hide what we really feel. Skillfully learning to articulate emotional range is a life's work. We'll offer you some assistance in dealing with some of this in our section on digital etiquette in death, but for now, it is important to realize that we are being called on to exercise these skills in the brave new world of the internet.

To deal with mourning on social media feeds we must not only become adept at responding to a sometimes confusing array of posts and comments — many that may be from relative strangers — we must also become adept at navigating the often emotionally charged content stream that will inevitably be interspersed with celebrity gossip, cat videos and mundane daily musings.

Crammed news feeds leave us bouncing from joy to sorrow without regard for the pace of our senses. We're left reeling, stranded in an algorithmically induced emotional storm. While social media is personal, the pace and scope of it is impersonal. As we mourn, it is important to remember that we each grieve at our own pace, and that pace is human. You may find it prudent to take some time offline when your grief is intense, or to ask a trusted friend to manage newsfeeds on your behalf.

On her blog, Vicki gets more personal on the subject of being human in a technical world. Read more here: www.vickimcleod. com/mindfulness/being-human-in-an-emoticon-world

5. Reliving Sad Memories

Being online may force you to confront your loss, or to relive sad memories, when you are least expecting it. As we have mentioned before, what happens in cyberspace is difficult to control. If you don't have a digital legacy plan enabling your loved ones to deal with your social media accounts, they will encounter these challenges as well. You risk becoming a digital zombie, a concept we introduced in Chapter 4. If social media accounts have not been properly memorialized or deleted, your profile will continue to be populated as though you are still living.

Many people we talked to while writing this book provided us with examples of coming across automated "wish so-and-so a happy birthday" reminder posts from Facebook. Said so-and-sos, of course being much-missed deceased friends, colleagues, or family members whose accounts are still active and haunting the social media feeds. Ubiquitous Memories posts or Friendversary reels are often untimely reminders of loss and sorrow. Almost universally, the people we spoke to found such posts disturbing, with many finding that they triggered new bouts of grief.

As the first generation that has had to deal with the interface of death and the digital age, we are in new territory and learning as we go. The platforms themselves are only just beginning to address the practical and technical aspects of dealing with social media accounts on behalf of the deceased. They still have a long way to go in terms of dealing with the social and emotional impacts of living and dying online.

6. Comfort in Self: Your Self-care Contract

Death takes a toll on the mourners. It can be an emotionally charged, stressful time filled with unfamiliar tasks. A long list of death-related action items added to your regular to-do list can be overwhelming. Grief brings out the best and the worst in family dynamics. The worst parts can add further strife to an already tender time. More than ever, it's essential that you take time for comfort to manage your stress, bolster your energy, and get all the necessary tasks done.

If you read Chapter 1, we hope that you took the time to create a personal Self-care Contract. If you missed this section, look back now and download a copy of the worksheet from the digital download kit, if desired. You'll recall this plan includes reminders for a variety of self-care strategies that work for you. You may have prioritized nutrition, sleep, solitude, companionship, distractions, exercise, or other approaches to help you get through this difficult time.

Assuming you are online or active on one or more social media platforms, reach out for one-to-one support from a trusted and loving friend via text, private message, or email. At times, dealing with the subject matter of this book rekindled memories loss and feelings of grief for both Vicki and Angela, never mind the usual stress of word counts and deadlines. Cheerful, kind, and encouraging private messages from friends, family, and colleagues helped ease us over the bumpy spots. There is power in your personal networks and it is one of the blessings of the digital age that we can so easily connect when needed.

7. Comfort in Community: Online Groups

Social media allows us the opportunity to create closed discussion groups, particularly using the Facebook Groups feature. A group on Facebook can be created to give a community a more private place to grieve. Depending on your situation, you may set up a group to connect those mourning a specific person. Another alternative is to join or create a group with others who have shared a similar loss such as stillbirth, death of a child, terminal cancer, unexpected death, death of a sibling, suicide, or other scenarios. Often shared experience groups are moderated by a professional counselor or an organization that supports the grieving.

> We are standing by to continue to support your digital legacy planning journey, and further the discussion on death and dying in the digital age. You are invited to join our Facebook Group, Death in the Digital Age at www.facebook.com/groups/311351059666776/.

Facebook Groups offers three privacy settings: public, private, and secret. Private and secret groups allow the administrator to control who joins the group by approving members. This creates a sense of safety, privacy, and intimacy amongst group members. Public groups are not recommended to gather those mourning a death as the information shared may be too personal for general consumption and the raw emotions expressed may draw unwanted comments from strangers or, worse, trolls.

For any such group to be successful, it is helpful to lay out some guidelines for participation. Be explicit in a pinned post that all members will see at the top of the group's newsfeed. That post could be used to note the name of the deceased, the circumstances of the person's death, and the types of posts encouraged in the group. A pinned post can also be used to define the scope of the group if membership includes those with shared experiences of a particular type of death. Typically, these sorts of groups outline what is not permitted in posts such as off-topic messages, sales or other solicitations, coarse language, explicit photographs, copyright infringements, or other criteria. It can also guide members with examples of the types of posts encouraged in the group, whether sharing emotions, cherished memories, requests for practical support, or more.

Whether the group focuses on an individual or a type of death, it is advisable to have one or more moderators oversee the group. The moderator can step in if a conversation turns to argument, offer outside resources if emotions are uncontrollable, or spurn any spammy content that members might share. In a digital legacy plan, your digital steward could act as moderator or can delegate the task to one or more willing community members.

The asynchronous nature of a Facebook Group can be helpful in grief. Group members can post at any time and any member can respond when they see the post. As grief can be amplified overnight and triggered at unexpected times, instant access to a supportive community is extremely helpful. Even if no one else is online when the post is made, the member knows that his or her voice will be heard and that responses are forthcoming.

Such a group is further advantageous because group members that live in distant locations can meet through social media without investing time or money in travel costs. As families and social groups can be spread around the world, the online space can act as a virtual living room for the group to hang out, just as they would if they all lived in the same neighborhood. Remember, even though we access it via technology, the internet is a place not a thing.

In addition, the group can become a source for practical support. Setting up childminding, eldercare transportation, shared meals, joint transportation, and more can be arranged in discussion without having to send a flurry of emails and texts to individuals hoping for help. Then a second or third round of emails canceling the request for assistance once someone has agreed to help. A group makes communication so much more efficient. Efficiency is vital during times of mourning and stress when people's patience and resources are stretched thin.

Groups that bond over a shared experience, such as the death of a loved one, form a tight knit community. In addition to understanding the context of requests and comments, group members develop a shared vocabulary; an in-group slang or shorthand that helps the group communicate efficiently. In Angela's family, the abbreviation GnG is used to denote Grannie and Grandad, for example.

While we've used Facebook Groups to illustrate our point, any communication tool shared amongst the bereaved and their supporters can be used in this way. If some members of your Group don't use Facebook, then consider group messaging in WhatsApp or repurpose a productivity tool such as Slack. WhatsApp and Slack are also platform-agnostic so there's no conflict between the iOS and Android users in your group. If the group is small, text messaging or email will work, too.

This approach to communication amongst a grief support group is supported by the research of Ylva Hard A Segerstad and Dick Kasperowski. In their article "A community for grieving: affordances of social media for support of bereaved parents," these researchers investigated a specific "closed peer grief support community on Facebook" and discovered benefits for the grieving parents in terms of the benefits of a closed community, shared experiences, flexible time to participate, and the accessibility of the group (*New Review of Hypermedia and Multimedia*, 2015).

8. Digital Etiquette in Death

The key to digital etiquette in death is to be real. By showing compassion and connecting on a human level, you won't commit a social faux pas when someone dies. How we interact online when someone is dying or has died, should be modeled on what we would do if we could be there in person. It's not unusual to feel awkward or unsure about what to say or how to act both online and offline. If your words and actions are well intentioned, then you're off to a good start.

That said, the very definition of polite behavior is evolving as our social interactions evolve to blend online and offline connections. Cards of condolence are no longer exclusively sent by post and may now appear as tweets, Facebook posts, blog comments, YouTube videos, or other digital expressions.

> When someone dies, it's customary to send a note of condolence. In this digital age, that might be a text message, email, social media comment, or other electronic communiqué. Although this is a digital time, it's still appropriate to go analog with a handwritten sympathy card sent as snail mail or delivered in person at the funeral or other memorial event.

A good condolence note, in either digital or analog form, includes five key elements:

- Start with a salutation, such as "Dear Mrs. Evans."

- Then, acknowledge the death. You might write, "I'm so sorry for your loss."

- Next, include a brief personal reflection on the deceased. Something like, "Ms. Smith was my favorite teacher" or "John was a gift to our community."

- Add an offer of support. You might write, "I will keep you in my prayers" or "Let me know if there's anything I can do to help."

- Finish with a closing such as "Sincerely" or "With deepest sympathy."

Be sure to send the note promptly after you learn of the death. It's easier on the bereaved to receive condolence notes near the date of death.

Part of the challenge is that while mourning etiquette is evolving, different people have different views of what's acceptable. In part, this may be generational (recall our discussion about legacy by the generations in Chapter 2) based on personal experiences with death as well as age, income level, and cultural influences. Digital life skills also come into play here as some are accustomed to digital as part of their day-to day-lives. If we acknowledge births, anniversaries, and weddings online, why wouldn't we address deaths, as well? Whatever the cause, the different beliefs on "proper" death etiquette can result in friction amongst family and friends.

Rather than leave you to muddle your way through how to behave with each death, the following reminders will help guide your words and your actions.

First and foremost, don't announce a death unless you are the closest connection to the deceased. If you are amongst the closest relatives or friends making the announcement decision, then consult with others who are near and dear to the departed to gain a consensus on when, or if, the death should be announced online.

Next, respect religious rituals and cultural traditions. For some, there may be one or more days of formal or private mourning for the family. In Jewish tradition, for example, first-degree family members (spouse, children, parents, and siblings), observe a week-long mourning period immediately after the body is buried. Sitting Shiva, as it's called, includes visits from friends and family. The decision to include or exclude digital visits through social media, texts, and emails will be decided by the family. The evolution of mourning visits has not yet reached consensus on whether this is appropriate or not so it's an individual decision. If you are part of the family, you'll have a say in the decision but if you are outside that inner group, you'll need to follow the family's lead.

Suppress your hurt feelings or anger if you find out about the death in a way that's uncomfortable for you. As we've said, It can be distressing to hear of death in your Facebook feed between celebrity gossip and cute cat videos, but those closest to the deceased can't fully control the distribution of the news. If someone shares it online publicly, you might see it. Don't add to the family's burden by piling your anger on top of their grief. Get support for your feelings elsewhere.

If you need professional support, reach out to Mental Health America (www.mentalhealthamerica.net/conditions/coping-loss-bereavement-and-grief), Canadian Mental Health Association (cmha.ca/documents/grieving), or similar organizations. They offer online resources and referrals to grief counselors in your area.

Take time to acknowledge that someone has died. Use technology to communicate after a death in the same ways you communicate with friends and family in life. If your primary communication channel with your best friend is text messaging, then continue to connect in that way. Sudden changes to communication channels can be stressful for the mourners. If you usually call, pick up the phone. If you usually email, open your computer. If you usually talk in person, pop in for a visit.

Don't forget to keep in touch. After you've acknowledged the death, check in with your friend or family member again at regular intervals. The closer you are to the deceased's inner circle, the more follow-up contacts are appropriate. Often, there is a flurry of support and assistance right after the death and through the funeral, celebration of life, or burial rituals. However, after that, mourning can be a lonely process. Grief doesn't end on a timeline and technology can be a great way to remind the living that you're still thinking of them. Sincere offers of companionship and assistance will be welcome and, in many cases, sharing memories and stories is a good way to move through grief.

As Dr. Kathy Kortes-Miller wrote in her book *Talking About Death Won't Kill You*, "We are still navigating the waters around dying, death, grief, and loss online" (ECW Press, 2018). While the social norms are evolving and adapting to technology, the ways we connect and communicate on a human level remain the same. Be real. Be kind. Be sincere. Be helpful.

9
The Social Shift: Death at the Intersection of Digital and Analog

Unlike physical death, where there are rituals and established practices to guide us, dealing with death in the digital age is a new phenomenon we've only had to cope with in the last two decades. Yet, looking forward, digital and death are inseparably intertwined from now on. We are the first generation on the planet that has had to grapple with the implications of crafting and curating billions of terabytes of data. Our children will become the stewards of our choices, and the keepers of our digital history. The time for your digital legacy plan is now.

We are in the midst of a massive social shift and nowhere is this more keenly felt than at the intersection of the digital and analog worlds. In addition to being the first generation dealing with death, dying, and legacy in the digital age, we are also the last generation to have known a world without the internet.

1. Everybody Dies: What's Your Plan?

Throughout this book, we've offered you information and guidance on how to create a digital legacy plan. The worksheets available in the digital download kit can be put together to document your plan. We hope you've taken time to get your digital affairs in order. Use the Digital Legacy Plan Checklist (shown in Sample 12) to make sure you have covered all your bases, and compile and keep everything together, either in a safe place in printed form or as a password-protected digital PDF file. Ensure a trusted loved one, or your executor has access.

Your digital legacy plan will, at a minimum, communicate your desires for your digital assets. Maybe you don't care what happens or you've made a detailed plan. Either way, your executor and/or digital steward will be grateful for the guidance you've provided. Knowing what matters to you and how to proceed will make their job much easier.

For sure, you've identified and secured any tangible value you have in your estate: PayPal balances, sales funnels, affiliate income, loyalty programs, and other assets that translate to the physical world. Along the way, you've probably organized the data you control and maybe even decluttered some of your information. Just as no one wants your old sock collection, a tidy digital footprint, like a tidy dresser, makes it easier to clean up after you are gone. It also lays the foundation for an actionable digital legacy plan.

As you live the rest of your life, we encourage you to revisit and update your plan from time to time. While a last will and testament tends to be a set it and forget it document that's only updated a few times in your life, a digital legacy plan needs constant updating to reflect additions and changes to your digital footprint. A few edits at regular intervals can be good for your well-being, too. It will relieve you of worrying about what happens to your digital stuff after death.

2. Social Responsibility: We're in It Together

While we have to deal with the digital options available today, we're also going to have to contemplate and form an opinion about

Sample 12
Digital Legacy Plan Checklist

<table>
<tr><td rowspan="2">**Digital Legacy Plan Checklist**</td><td colspan="2">Date: December 16, 2019</td></tr>
<tr><td colspan="2">Use this worksheet to review the status of your digital legacy plan.</td></tr>
<tr><td>Have I completed a Self-care Plan? Am I ready to undertake the task of digital legacy planning?</td><td>☒ Yes
☐ No</td></tr>
<tr><td>Have I completed the Your Digital Life Worksheet, so I understand my digital values?</td><td>☒ Yes
☐ No</td></tr>
<tr><td>Have I completed the Digital Assets Inventory Worksheet?</td><td>☒ Yes
☐ No</td></tr>
<tr><td>Have I compiled and scanned all important related documents that may be still in analog form (e.g., birth certificate, marriage certificate, business incorporation papers)?</td><td>☒ Yes
☐ No</td></tr>
<tr><td>If I am acting on behalf of someone else, do I have all the documentation I need in order to prove my relationship to him or her and proof of death, (e.g., death certificate, obituary, etc.)?</td><td>☐ Yes
☒ No</td></tr>
<tr><td>Have I noted the name and contact information of my lawyer, notary, IT contact, and executor?</td><td>☐ Yes
☒ No</td></tr>
<tr><td>Have I identified, named, and notified someone to act as my digital steward?</td><td>☐ Yes
☒ No</td></tr>
<tr><td>Have I gone through my social media and other online accounts and ensured the appropriate legacy contacts have been named (where possible), or that my wishes are written down for each account?</td><td>☐ Yes
☒ No</td></tr>
<tr><td>If I am acting on behalf of another, or writing my own premortem obituary, have I identified what parts of my digital content are important, using the Privacy Preferences Worksheet?</td><td>☒ Yes
☐ No</td></tr>
<tr><td>Have I created and crafted a timeline of important life milestones to be included in notices and obituaries?</td><td>☐ Yes
☒ No</td></tr>
<tr><td>Have I sufficiently decluttered my data to make it easy for my loved ones to deal with my digital legacy after I am gone?</td><td>☐ Yes
☒ No</td></tr>
<tr><td>Have I had a conversation with my loved ones about my wishes in regard to digital legacy planning?</td><td>☒ Yes
☐ No</td></tr>
<tr><td>Have I spoken to my executor and/or digital steward about my digital legacy planning wishes?</td><td>☐ Yes
☒ No</td></tr>
<tr><td>Have I compiled all my digital legacy plan documents in one place – online or offline or both – to ensure the information is readily available?</td><td>☐ Yes
☒ No</td></tr>
</table>

technologies in development driven by artificial intelligence (AI). Is the future going to be filled with animated, responsive avatars that replicate our living, digitally immortal selves? Will data storage find a way to capture all the memories in our brains and make them accessible on a server? Will we be cloned into robot form like Twiki in *Buck Rogers in the 25th Century*? As digital advancements progress, will society simply accept all possible digital legacy or will we protest en masse at some point? Or will we stay present and focus only on what's happening in the now — online and off?

As early adopters in the digital age, both Angela and Vicki are somewhat ahead of the general population in terms of looking at and dealing with issues like digital legacy. Nevertheless, writing this book forced us to take a hard look at our own choices in regard to digital immortality. As we try to illustrate in this book, much depends on personal preference and digital habits, the degree or need for control after you are gone, your generation, and the sense of importance you have about your contribution to the world at large. Your family or cultural feelings about legacy, history, and genealogy will also come into play.

Vicki was born near the end of the 1950s. She's a baby boomer. As an advocate for happiness, mindfulness, and living a passionate and engaged life (online and off) she believes first and foremost that how we live our daily lives is what matters. As a coach and consultant she has spent a lifetime career supporting leaders in governments, organizations, and businesses to engage in meaningful strategies for positive change, including how to engage ethically in the digital space. She believes her legacy largely rests in the work she has done and the influence she has had on the lives she has touched, in real life or virtually. As a writer and artist, it is important to her that her creative work lives on through her books, poetry, essays, columns, and blogs, but it is not as important to her that her persona exists beyond her natural lifetime. Vicki and her husband have no children. On her side, the family does not have a large attachment to ancestral legacy, or family history. Vicki's grandparents and great-grandparents emigrated to Canada to start a new life and purposefully left behind their old life. For Vicki, securing her digital legacy means preserving her creative work, sustaining the communities it serves, and ensuring an easy and efficient transition for her loved ones after she is gone. Having said that, being naturally curious, Vicki is not opposed to experimenting with the creation of a social robot or avatar, just for the sake of seeing what that's all about!

In contrast, Angela was born in the 1970s. She's part of Generation X, the generation that pioneered digital living. Angela advocates for an integrated digital life; one where we embrace and use technology in ways that enhance our life while being open to a healthy balance with analog activities. As an author and educator, Angela helps individuals and organizations learn the digital life skills needed to achieve this balance. Angela doesn't yet think of her life's work as a legacy but she knows that she's made significant contributions in research, writing, and teaching that have influenced thousands. Angela's digital footprint is a combination of community and content. These elements work together to support her friendships, working relationships, and connections with fans. Family is paramount to Angela and her digital legacy includes not only her own stories but the history of generations before her. She finds joy in capturing stories such as the family connection to the

Fairmont Banff Springs Hotel in the 1920s and the World War II romance of her grandparents. She's also thoughtfully documenting her son's life through social media. Collectively, her professional work, the revenue it generates, and her personal memoirs are the most important elements of her digital legacy today. As technology advances, Angela will be on the forefront exploring the potential and the implications for herself and others.

Our wish for you, dear reader, is that you will find this book a useful guide as you travel the somewhat difficult territory of planning your own digital legacy, or acting on behalf of someone while you or they are grieving. We hope it has inspired you to take this journey in a mindful way, with patience and gentleness, and to be a diligent steward of your assets now, so it will be easier for your loved ones later. If you are mourning, we hope we have offered you some direction and some comfort.

As authors and colleagues, we share a commitment to being fully human in a digital world. We offer this book as a roadmap to navigating the very specific intersection where we find ourselves, the crossroads of death and dying in the digital age. We are in this together. We're honored to share the road.

Download Kit

Please enter the URL you see in the box below into a web browser on your computer to access and use the download kit.

www.self-counsel.com/updates/dlegacy/19kit.htm

The following resources are included on the download kit:

- Self-care Plan Worksheet
- Your Digital Life Worksheet
- Digital Assets Inventory Worksheet
- Important Contacts Worksheet
- Clean Your Digital Closet Worksheet
- Social Media and Other Accounts Worksheet
- Writing an Obituary Worksheet
- Personal Milestones Worksheet
- Privacy Preferences Worksheet

- Museum of Me Worksheet
- Personal Reflections on Death and Dying Worksheet
- Digital Legacy Plan Worksheet